Matching Reading Data to Interventions

This accessible and reader-friendly book will help you assess and determine the foundational reading needs of each of your K – 5 students. Literacy leaders Jill Dunlap Brown and Jana Schmidt offer an easy-to-use data analysis tool called, "The Columns" for teachers at all levels of experience to make sense of classroom data for elementary readers. This book will guide you in using the tool to identify the root causes of foundational reading deficits and to plan appropriate interventions. Sample case studies allow you to practice identifying needs and matching interventions. Stories and examples throughout the book will encourage you as you help your students meet their full potential.

The book provides easy-to-use and printable versions of the data analysis columns that will enable you to put the authors' advice into immediate action. These tools are available for download on the book's product page: www.routledge.com/9780367225070

Jill Dunlap Brown has worked in the field of education for 20 years and now serves as Assistant Superintendent for Elementary Education in a school district of 19,000 students.

Jana Schmidt has worked as an associate director in the Educational Leadership and Policy Analysis Department at the University of Missouri-Columbia and as an educational consultant. Jana has served as a language arts coordinator for kindergarten through eighth grade in a school district with approximately 19,000 students.

**Other Eye On Education Books
Available from Routledge**
(www.routledge.com/eyeoneducation)

**Passionate Learners, 2nd Edition
How to Engage and Empower Your Students**
Pernille Ripp

**Passionate Readers
The Art of Reaching and Engaging Every Child**
Pernille Ripp

**The Common Core Grammar Toolkit
Using Mentor Texts to Teach the Language Standards in Grades 9-12**
Sean Ruday

**The First-Year English Teacher's Guidebook
Strategies for Success**
Sean Ruday

Culturally Relevant Teaching in the English Language Arts Classroom
Sean Ruday

Essential Truths for Teachers
Danny Steele and Todd Whitaker

Matching Reading Data to Interventions

A Simple Tool for Elementary Educators

Jill Dunlap Brown and Jana Schmidt

Routledge
Taylor & Francis Group
NEW YORK AND LONDON

First published 2020
by Routledge
52 Vanderbilt Avenue, New York, NY 10017

and by Routledge
2 Park Square, Milton Park, Abingdon, Oxon, OX14 4RN

Routledge is an imprint of the Taylor & Francis Group, an informa business

© 2020 Taylor & Francis

The right of Jill Dunlap Brown and Jana Schmidt to be identified as authors of this work has been asserted by them in accordance with sections 77 and 78 of the Copyright, Designs and Patents Act 1988.

All rights reserved. No part of this book may be reprinted or reproduced or utilised in any form or by any electronic, mechanical, or other means, now known or hereafter invented, including photocopying and recording, or in any information storage or retrieval system, without permission in writing from the publishers.

Trademark notice: Product or corporate names may be trademarks or registered trademarks, and are used only for identification and explanation without intent to infringe.

Library of Congress Cataloging-in-Publication Data
A catalog record for this title has been requested

ISBN: 978-0-367-22506-3 (hbk)
ISBN: 978-0-367-22507-0 (pbk)
ISBN: 978-0-429-27523-4 (ebk)

Typeset in Palatino
by Swales & Willis, Exeter, Devon, UK

Visit the eResources: www.routledge.com/9780367225070

The Columns © Jill Dunlap Brown and Jana Schmidt. Used with permission.

Contents

Meet the Authors..viii
eResources.. x

1 An Overview of The Columns 1
What Are The Columns? 2
Why Are Kindergarten and First Grade Discussed in Their Own
  Chapter? 14
Can We Use The Columns with Our English Language
Learners and Special Education Students? 15
How Might The Columns Be Helpful for Administrators? 15

2 Kindergarten and The Columns 17
Column 1 in Kindergarten 18
Column 2 in Kindergarten 19
Column 3 in Kindergarten 19
Column 4 in Kindergarten 20
Column 5 in Kindergarten 21
Frequently Asked Questions for Kindergarten 22

3 Grade 1 and The Columns 25
First Grade, First Semester: Column 1 – High Phonological/
  Phonemic Awareness, High Phonics 25
First Grade, First Semester: Columns 2–6 Overview 26
First Grade, First Semester: Columns 2–6 – A Range in
  Phonological/Phonemic Awareness Ability 27
First Grade, First Semester: Columns 2–6 – A Range in
  Phonics Ability 28
First Grade, Second Semester 30
First Grade, Second Semester: Column 1 – Meets or Exceeds
  Fluency Benchmark Scores 30
First Grade, Second Semester: Column 2 30
First Grade, Second Semester: Columns 3 and 4 31
Frequently Asked Questions for First Grade 32

4 Column 1 for Grades 2–5: A Focus on Comprehension and Standards 34
The Top of Column 1 for Grades 2–5 34
Instruction for Students at the Top of Column 1 35
Students in the Lower Section of Column 1 37
Intervening with Students in the Lower Section of Column 1 37
One Extra Caveat for Fourth and Fifth Grades 38
Frequently Asked Questions for Column 1 in Grades 2–5 38

5 Column 2 for Grades 2–5 41
The Importance of Fluency in the Reading Process 41
Column 2 for Grades 2–5 42
Distinguishing Phonics and Fluency Needs 42
Hooking Assessment Information to Intervention 44
Frequently Asked Questions about Column 2 45

6 Column 3 for Grades 2–5 47
The Importance of Phonics in the Reading Process 47
Column 3 for Grades 2–5 48
Frequently Asked Questions about Column 3 51

7 Column 4 for Grades 2–5 55
Working with Our Most Struggling Learners 55
The Steps for this Column Mirror Column 3 57
How Do We Intervene for These Students? 57
Frequently Asked Questions for Column 4 58

8 Case Studies for Each Grade Level 59
Kindergarten Case Study 61
First Grade Case Study 70
Second Grade Case Study 93
Third Grade Case Study 105
Fourth Grade Case Study 117
Fifth Grade Case Study 130
Final Thoughts about The Columns Tool 142

9 A Guide to Columns Implementation 143
How Can I Get The Columns Process Underway? 143
How Can I Use The Columns with My Team? 145

For Administrators: Suggestions for How to Use The
    Columns in Your School or District..........................145
In Conclusion 146

References 147

Meet the Authors

Jill Dunlap Brown, PhD

Jill began her career as a second and third grade teacher, and later spent time as a literacy coach. She spent 7 years as an educational consultant for schools across Missouri. She assisted schools with understanding the components of reading, reading data, and reading interventions. She also assisted schools in implementing RTI as a system, and development of curriculum around state standards. She spent 5 years as an elementary principal and now serves as Assistant Superintendent for Elementary Education in a school district of 19,000 students.

Jill has worked in the field of education for 20 years. During these years, she has worked with students, teachers, administrators, universities, and state departments. Her passion is ensuring that all children learn to read and that every teacher is empowered to know how to ensure this happens.

Jill holds a BA in Elementary Education, a MEd in Curriculum and Instruction, an EdS in Educational Leadership and Policy Analysis, and a PhD in Educational Leadership and Policy Analysis.

Jana Schmidt, EdS

Through various aspects of education, Jana Schmidt has had the privilege of working with educators and students from multiple school districts. Jana served as an associate director in the Educational Leadership and Policy Analysis department at the University of Missouri-Columbia. There she worked to structure professional development and outreach efforts for superintendents, principals, teachers, and other educators throughout the state. Through the University of Missouri and at times in conjunction with programs from the Missouri Department of Elementary and Secondary Education, she served as an educational consultant providing interaction with national presenters, organizing state collaboratives, presenting school-based professional development, and facilitating school professional learning teams. The focus of these efforts included literacy, systems of support, response to intervention, work with standards and assessment, and development of school leaders. Jana served in this capacity for 16 years.

Jana has also served as a language arts coordinator for kindergarten through eighth grade in a school district of 19,000 students. At the beginning of her career, Jana taught second grade, third grade, and reading classes. Jana's overall career spans over 25 years.

Her educational path includes a BSEd in Elementary Education, MEd in Reading Education, and an EdS in Educational Leadership and Policy Analysis.

eResources

The Columns in this book can also be downloaded and printed for classroom use. You can access these downloads by visiting the book product page on our website: www.routledge.com/9780367225070. Then click on the tab that says "eResources," and select the files. They will begin downloading to your computer.

1
An Overview of The Columns

"I have all of this great data about my students, but I'm not sure what to do next!" It's a sentence we have heard over and over again as we have worked in schools for the past 20 years. Teachers spend time screening students and collecting data, but the power of data comes at the next stage – the stage of identifying the foundational reading need and then matching students to an intervention that will help them become successful readers. This is the link between what we know to do (the research) and the actual work in school. Many call this the "Knowing–Doing Gap" (Sparks, 2007, pp. 179–184). We know what we should do, but how do we actually do it? The implementation behind the work is difficult. We have spent many hours in data teams with teachers who are eager to do more and understand more so that they can help their students. Because of this need, we developed an assessment analysis tool that we call "The Columns." The Columns provide teachers with a tool that assists in identifying the foundational reading needs of students in their classrooms. This tool is meant to help teachers understand what foundational reading skill is missing so that the student is placed in the proper reading intervention. We base The Columns on the five components of reading. We know that for a child to be a successful reader, they must be proficient in phonological awareness, phonics, fluency, vocabulary, and comprehension. For teachers to best meet the needs of students, they must be able to identify which components are strong and which are weak, thus allowing them to know the next steps that are required for each child.

The Columns guide the teacher's thinking as they dissect collected data. The one thing we have learned over the years is that the process must be kept simple. The one thing no teacher has more of is time. Between teaching all the subjects, knowing all the standards, tending to needs of children, recess duty, lunch duty, calls to parents, and many meetings, teachers need a process that is quick, efficient, and gives them exactly the information essential to ensuring the foundational reading needs of their students are met. We worked for many years to create just this – a process that is easy to understand and a guide that is easy to implement. In this chapter, we will share The Columns and provide an overview of what teachers will find when using The Columns for foundational reading data analysis, as well as how The Columns can be helpful for administrators. In the subsequent chapters, teachers will be given the tools to understand how The Columns work for kindergarten, first grade, and grades 2 through 5. We will explain the nuances of each, and the decisions that a teacher makes as deficient skills in foundational reading are realized. To see what The Columns look like, please turn to page 4.

What Are The Columns?

The Columns were developed to provide an efficient data analysis tool to help identify the foundational reading skill that might be missing, and then match that deficient skill to an intervention. They are set up in a simple format that allows the teacher to read the data decision rules in each Column. Then the tool helps to guide the teacher to determine what foundational reading skill might be missing, and finally, references the intervention that matches the deficit. While in this book we discuss both universal screening assessment tools and interventions that might be used, the power of The Columns is that they are adaptable to data tools and interventions that your school might use. We know that there are many choices for reading screeners and interventions. It is not our intention to promote one tool or program over another, but rather to help schools to best use the tools they have selected and identify which intervention matches the foundational reading skill deficit that is found in the data collected. Often times, schools have many interventions available, but may not know how to match the intervention to the need. Our tool will help you decide how to place interventions you currently use into The Columns to ensure students are matched to the correct intervention. Further, it will help you identify where you might need additional interventions for students. The tools and interventions we mention in this book are those we have used in schools over the years. We know there are many choices for schools. We hope this tool helps you align what you have and also identifies what might still be needed. Gaps in foundational reading knowledge will surface when collecting student data.

The Columns are available for each grade level, K-5. We devote one chapter to just kindergarten and one to first grade, to be able to address the beginning phases of reading. For kindergarten, there are five Columns for analysis. Grade 1 has six Columns for the first semester, and then it is reduced to four Columns for the second semester. Grades 2–5 have four Columns focused on expanding the knowledge of those learners. In total, a school will have four sets of Columns for grades K-5.

Each Column begins by using the data from a universal screener. At the beginning of each school year, teachers give a universal screening assessment to all students in their classroom. This is typically done for all students again in mid-year, and again at the end of the year. Over time, growth is measured for students. Your school might use AIMSweb, Acadience (formerly DIBELS), Fastbridge, iReady, or another research-based universal screening tool. These tools will give you a percentile score. Once teachers have placed students in Columns by using this percentile indicator, The Columns then guide you through the next steps as you think about what intervention might be best for that student, based on the data just collected. Each Column requires a teacher to rule out or confirm the need identified in that Column. Let's review an example that will be discussed in more detail in Chapter 4 for grades 2–5.

A second grade teacher has used the universal screener and identified the percentile score on the assessment. The teacher refers to the grades 2–5 set of Columns and knows to initially place the child in Column 2. Once the teacher has determined the initial Column placement, the directions in The Column will prompt the teacher to do further assessments to confirm or reject the need for the student to remain in that Column. Further testing, with the correct diagnostic assessment (something we will discuss in the chapters to come), allows the teacher to determine if the universal screener has lead to identification of the correct deficient skill. It also provides further information about the specific skills students need assistance with. If, after additional assessment, the second grade student remains in Column 2, the teacher can be sure there is a need for an intervention in the reading component of fluency. The Columns would then suggest an intervention related to this component. We will provide more detail about this process as we discuss The Columns for grades 2–5.

1. Kindergarten Columns
2. First grade, first semester Columns
3. First grade, second semester Columns
4. Second through fifth grade Columns
5. Columns clarifications

Kindergarten Columns

Column 1: Ready to read – phonics, short vowels plus CVC
Students in this column have mastered letters, letter sounds and phonemic awareness skills.

Universal screener:
- Letter naming fluency at/above 40th percentile
- Letter sound fluency at/above 40th percentile
- Phoneme segmentation at/above 40th percentile
- Initial sound fluency at/above 40th percentile
- Composite score above 40th percentile

Possible enrichment (examples):
- Sound Partners Kindergarten
- Fundations

Your enrichment tools here:

Student names:

Column 2: Need letter naming
Students in this column cannot identify some or all letters.

Universal screener:
- Letter naming fluency below 40th percentile

Skill checklist:
___ Makes random errors
___ Errors on upper-case letters
___ Errors on lower-case letters
___ Errors on letters going below the line
___ Errors in letters in student's name
___ Doesn't track correctly
___ Return sweep
___ Consistent error on a specific letter

Possible interventions (examples):
- Fundations (matched to student need)
- www.fcrr.org
- Sound Partners Kindergarten
- Orton-Gillingham

Your intervention tools here:

Student names:

Column 3: Need letter sounds
Students in this column do not know some or all letter sounds.

Universal screener:
- Letter sound fluency below 40th percentile

Skill checklist:
___ Makes random errors
___ Errors on lower-case letters
___ Errors on letters going below the line
___ Errors in letters in student's name
___ Doesn't track correctly
___ Return sweep
___ Consistent error on a specific letter

Possible interventions (examples):
- Fundations (matched to student need)
- www.fcrr.org
- Sound Partners Kindergarten
- Orton-Gillingham

Your intervention tools here:

Student names:

Column 4: Need phonological awareness	Column 5: Need high frequency words	Teacher notes here:
Students in this column need help with phonemic awareness skills **Universal screener:** ◆ Phoneme segmentation below 40th percentile ◆ Initial sound fluency below 40th percentile **Skill checklist:** ___ Concept of word ___ Rhyming words ___ Syllables ___ Onset/rime ___ Isolation of initial sounds ___ Isolation of middle sounds ___ Isolation of final sounds ___ Blending ___ Segmenting ___ Addition ___ Substitution ___ Deletion **Possible interventions (examples):** ◆ Heggerty ◆ www.fcrr.org ◆ LiPS **Your intervention tools here:** **Student names:**	Students in this column need support in identifying and application of basic sight words. **Student names:**	

First Grade, First Semester

Column 1: Need to extend phonics work plus comprehension/standards work
Students in this column have phonological awareness and beginning phonics skills. These students can work on comprehension skills, extend farther into the phonics skills sequence beyond current grade level instruction, and make application to text with those new skills.

For students in this column, complete the universal screener:
- Example: Phoneme segmentation fluency at/above 40th percentile
- Example: Nonsense word fluency at/above 40th percentile
- Example: Composite score at/above 40th percentile

Instructional focus: Application to text; identify comprehension skill; next phonics need in skills sequence

Possible enrichments (examples):
- Application to text

Your enrichment tools here:

Student names:

Column 2: Need beginning phonics and application to text
Students in this column have phonological awareness skills, but need to work on beginning phonics. Kids falling in this column will have different phonics needs. You will determine where the student falls within the scope and sequence of phonics. Once this is determined, you should group students according to these phonics skills.

For students in this column, complete the universal screener:
- Example: Phoneme segmentation fluency at/above 40th percentile
- Example: Nonsense word fluency below the 40th percentile

Next steps:
- Complete the phonics survey to pinpoint where students are in the scope and sequence of phonics

Instructional focus: Phonics skill building; application of known phonics skills to text

Possible interventions (examples) (use guidelines of the intervention to find beginning instruction based on phonics survey):
- Fundations
- Sound Partners
- www.fcrr.org

Your intervention tools here:

Student names:

Column 3: Need phonological awareness, has basic phonics Students in this column master basic phonics skills. There is a deficit in phonological awareness skills.	**Column 4: Need phonics and phonological awareness skills** Students in this column are low in both phonics and phonological awareness skills. **A distinction for this column is that students fall in the 25th through 39th percentiles in phonics.**
For students in this column, complete the universal screener: ◆ Example: Phoneme segmentation fluency below 40th percentile ◆ Example: Nonsense word fluency above 40th percentile	**For students in this column, complete the universal screener:** ◆ Example: Phoneme segmentation fluency below 40th percentile ◆ Example: Nonsense word fluency between 25th and 39th percentiles
Next steps: ◆ Complete the phonological awareness diagnostic to pinpoint where students are in the scope and sequence of phonological awareness	**Next steps:** ◆ Complete the phonics survey to pinpoint where students are in the scope and sequence of phonics ◆ Complete the phonological awareness diagnostic to pinpoint where students are in the scope and sequence of phonological awareness
Instructional focus: Specific skills in the phonological awareness scope and sequence	**Instructional focus:** Phonics skill building; application of known phonics skills to text
Possible interventions (examples) (use guidelines of the intervention to find beginning instruction based on PA diagnostic): ◆ Phonological awareness: Heggerty; fcrr.org; LiPS	**Possible interventions (examples) (use guidelines of the intervention to find beginning instruction based on phonics survey and PA diagnostic):** ◆ Phonological awareness: Heggerty; fcrr.org; LiPS ◆ Phonics: Fundations; Sound Partners; Wilson Reading System; Barton Reading; Orton-Gillingham
Your intervention tools here:	**Your intervention tools here:**
Student names:	**Student names:**

Column 5: Need basic phonics and phonological awareness
Students in this column are low in both phonics and phonological awareness skills. Students know letters and letter sounds. **A distinction is that students in this column fall in between the 11th and 24th percentiles in phonics.**

For students in this column, complete the universal screener:
- Example: Phoneme segmentation fluency below 40th percentile
- Example: Nonsense word fluency between 11th and 24th percentiles

Next steps:
- Complete the phonics survey to pinpoint where students are in the scope and sequence of phonics
- Complete the phonological awareness diagnostic to pinpoint where students are in the scope and sequence of phonological awareness

Instructional focus: Specific skills in phonics and phonological awareness scope and sequence

Possible interventions (examples) (use guidelines of the intervention to find beginning instruction based on phonics survey and PA diagnostic):
- Phonics: Fundations; Sound Partners; Orton-Gillingham
- Phonological awareness: Heggerty; fcrr.org; LiPS

Your intervention tools here:

Student names:

Column 6: May meed work with letter identification and letter sounds plus very beginning phonics plus phonological awareness
Students in this column may need support with identifying some letters and/or letter sounds. They need support with phonological awareness and the very beginning skills in the phonics sequence. **A distinction is that students in this column fall below the 10th percentile in phonics.**

For students in this column, complete the universal screener:
- Example: Phoneme segmentation fluency below 40th percentile
- Example: AIMSweb nonsense word fluency below 10th percentile

Next steps:
- Complete the phonics survey to pinpoint where students are in the scope and sequence of phonics
- Complete the phonological awareness diagnostic to pinpoint where students are in the scope and sequence of phonological awareness
- If letter naming fluency and letter sound fluency are not included in the phonics survey or phonological awareness diagnostic, then administer separately

Instructional focus: Letter identification and letter sound; specific skills in phonological awareness scope and sequence

Possible interventions (examples):
- Phonics: Fundations; LiPS; letter recognition and letter/sound correspondence; Wilson Reading System; Barton Reading; Orton-Gillingham
- Phonological awareness: Heggerty

Your intervention tools here:

Student names:

First Grade, Second Semester

Column 1: Need to extend phonics work plus comprehension/standards work

Students in this column have phonemic awareness and beginning phonics skills. These children are able to read connected text at an appropriate rate according to grade level assessment. They are fluent. These students can work on comprehension skills, extend farther into the phonics skills sequence beyond current grade level instruction, and make application to text with those new skills.

For students in this column, complete the universal screener:
- Example: AIMSweb oral reading at/above 40th percentile
- Example: Composite score at/above 40th percentile

Instructional focus: Application to text; identify comprehension skill; next phonics need in skills sequence

Possible enrichment (example):
- Application to text

Your intervention tools here:

Student names:

Column 2: Need beginning phonics and application to text

Students in this column have phonemic awareness skills. They mastered some basic phonics skills, but are low in rate of fluency. They need to fluently read the phonics skills that they have mastered. Determine where the student falls within the scope and sequence of phonics. Once this is determined, you should group students according to these phonics skills and work to increase fluent application of phonics and decoding skills to text.

For students in this column, complete the universal screener:
- Example: AIMSweb oral reading between 25th and 39th percentiles
- Example: Composite score between 25th and 39th percentiles

Next steps:
- Complete the phonics survey – no phonics concerns should be found for Column 2
- Complete the phonological awareness diagnostic – no concerns should be found for Column 2

Instructional focus: Application of known phonics skills to text; increase in rate of fluency

Possible interventions (examples):
- Fundations
- www.fcrr.org

Your intervention tools here:

Student names:

Column 3: Need basic phonics and possibly phonological awareness skills Students in this column are low in both phonics and phonemic awareness skills. Students have not mastered some basic phonics skills. Students know letters and letter sounds.	**Column 4: Need work with letter identification and letter sounds** Students in this column need support with identifying some letters and/or letter sounds. They also need support with phonological awareness.
For students in this column, complete the universal screener: ◆ Example: AIMSweb oral reading between 11th and 24th percentiles ◆ Example: Composite score between 11th and 24th percentiles	**For students in this column, complete the universal screener:** ◆ Example: AIMSweb oral reading below 10th percentile ◆ Example: Composite score below 10th percentile
Next steps: ◆ Complete the phonics survey to pinpoint where students are in the scope and sequence of phonics ◆ Complete the phonological awareness diagnostic to pinpoint where students are in the scope and sequence of phonological awareness	**Next steps:** ◆ Complete the phonics survey to pinpoint where students are in the scope and sequence of phonics ◆ Complete the phonological awareness diagnostic to pinpoint where students are in the scope and sequence of phonological awareness
Instructional focus: Specific skills in phonics and phonological awareness scope and sequence	**Instructional focus:** Specific skills in the phonological awareness scope and sequence; fluency of letter identification and letter sound
Possible interventions (examples): ◆ Phonics: Sound Partners; Fundations; Orton-Gillingham ◆ Phonological awareness: Heggerty; www.fcrr.org (match need to areas of deficit on the phonological awareness survey); LiPS	**Possible interventions (examples):** ◆ Phonics: Sound Partners; Fundations; letter recognition and letter/sound correspondence; Wilson Reading System; Barton Reading; Orton-Gillingham ◆ Phonological awareness: Heggerty; LiPS
Your intervention tools here:	**Your intervention tools here:**
Student names – phonics only: **Student names – phonics and phonological awareness:**	**Student names:**

Second Through Fifth Grade Columns

Column 1: Comprehension/standards work needed – students are fluent and accurate
Students in this column have phonics, are fluent readers, but
need to continue to work on grade level standards.

For students in this column, complete the universal screener:
- Example: Oral reading fluency at/above 40th percentile
- Example: Composite score at/above 40th percentile

To identify the instructional focus:
- Common formative assessments aligned to state standards
- Vocabulary if your screener assesses this component

Possible enrichments (top of the column)/ interventions (bottom of the column) (examples):
- Standards work-identified prioritized standards
- Vocabulary
- Student's next steps may be enrichment related to the standards OR it could be intervention on basic comprehension plus standards work (PALS, Making Meaning, Strategies that Work Toolkit)
- Standards-based websites

**Student names of those proficient with basic comprehension,
but should work on standards:**

Student names of those that are fluent, but struggle with basic comprehension (they also need standards work):

Column 2: Fluency needed – accurate and slow
Students in this column have basic phonics skills, but read slowly.

For students in this column, complete the universal screener:
- Example: Oral reading fluency between 25th and 39th percentiles
- Example: Composite score between 25th and 39th percentiles

Next steps:
- To be in this column, phonics must be ruled out as a barrier to fluency. A phonics survey should be completed. If this survey reveals holes in phonics mastery, the student should be moved to Column 3

Fluency skills to consider:
_____Reads word by word
_____Reads with some phrasing
_____Speed reads the passage
_____Adjusts rate for comprehension
_____Rate impacts accuracy

Possible intervention (example):
- Read Naturally

Your intervention tools here:

Student names:

Column 3: Phonics needed, possibly phonological awareness	**Column 4: Phonics needed, phonological awareness needed**
Students in this column need direct, explicit instruction in phonics skills and in application of phonics in connected text.	Students in this column need direct, explicit instruction in phonics and phonological awareness.

Column 3:

For students in this column, complete the universal screener:
- Example: Oral reading fluency between 11th and 24th percentiles
- Example: Composite score between 11th and 24th percentiles
- Students in Column 2 found to have phonics concerns as determined by a phonics survey will be moved to Column 3

Next steps:
- Complete the phonics survey to pinpoint where students are in the scope and sequence of phonics
- Complete the phonological awareness diagnostic to rule out a phonological deficit OR confirm the deficit to determine the instructional focus

Possible interventions (examples):
- Phonics: Sound Partners; Fundations
- Phonological awareness: Heggerty; www.fcrr.org (match need to areas of deficit on the phonological awareness survey); LiPS

Your intervention tools here:

Student names – phonics only:

Student names – phonics and phonological awareness:

Column 4:

For students in this column, complete the universal screener:
- Example: Oral reading fluency below 10th percentile
- Example: Composite score below 10th percentile

Next steps:
- Complete the phonics survey to pinpoint where students are in the scope and sequence of phonics – identify the instructional focus
- Complete the phonological awareness diagnostic to identify needs within the scope and sequence of phonological awareness
- It is possible students in this column could pass the phonological awareness diagnostic. If they do, they will only require phonics intervention

Possible interventions (examples):
- Phonics: Sound Partners; Fundations; Wilson Reading System; Barton Reading; Orton-Gillingham
- Phonological awareness: Heggerty; www.fcrr.org (match need to areas of deficit on the phonological awareness diagnostic); LiPS

Your intervention tools here:

Student names – phonics only:

Student names – phonics and phonological awareness:

Columns Clarifications

Columns Clarifications
Phonological Awareness Explanation Plus Scope and Sequence: For further information, the Common Core State Standards Appendix A has a general explanation of the sequence of skills in phonological awareness. To access this information go to the following link and refer to pages 17–19: http://www.corestandards.org/assets/Appendix_A.pdf

Columns Clarifications
Phonological Diagnostic Assessment: A phonological diagnostic assessment is a tool that will help you identify a student's strengths and weaknesses within the phonological scope and sequence. It will pinpoint where to begin phonological instruction.

Columns Clarifications
Phonics Explanation Plus Scope and Sequence: For further information, the Common Core State Standards Appendix A has a general explanation of the sequence of skills in phonics. To access this information go to the following link and refer to pages 20–22: http://www.corestandards.org/assets/Appendix_A.pdf

Columns Clarifications
Phonics Survey: A phonics survey is a tool that will help you identify a student's strengths and weaknesses within the phonics scope and sequence. It will pinpoint where to begin instruction.

As you study The Columns, you will see a few interventions listed on each one. These are simply ideas that stem from interventions we have used in schools over the years. What is great about this tool is that you add the interventions you have available. This tool is designed to ensure you match the correct intervention to the correct foundational reading deficit. It is our hope that The Columns will assist your teachers with identifying the missing foundational reading skill, and then provide support by matching the skill to the intervention that your school utilizes. We like to think of our tool as the bridge for the knowing and doing gap. This tool is meant to help the teacher identify the missing foundational reading skill and locate the intervention that might work best.

The power of The Columns is the simplicity of the step-by-step guide for teachers as they think through the foundational reading needs for each student. This tool takes away the guessing of what the foundational reading deficit might be and what intervention might be best. Gone are the days of going to the shelf and choosing an intervention that looks like a good fit. The Columns are the data process that links screening and intervention together. Through the decision-making process that is The Columns, multiple factors will be considered by teachers related to the needs of each individual student, ensuring the teacher feels confident that the child is getting just what they need to become a skilled reader.

Why Are Kindergarten and First Grade Discussed in Their Own Chapter?

We take time to delve into kindergarten and first grade by devoting these chapters to our youngest learners. Some students enter kindergarten able to read, and others do not yet know names of letters. We developed The Columns in kindergarten to concentrate in part on the very discreet foundational reading skills to determine where a child is in their understanding of the alphabetic principle. The alphabetic principle is the understanding that systematic and predictable relationships exist between written letters and spoken sounds (Texas Education Agency, 2002). In simple terms, letters and sounds go together to produce a word. While this concept seems simple, there are many skills that must be monitored to ensure a child has strong alphabetic principle. The student must know letter names, letter sounds, and must have a firm foundation of phonological awareness. The teacher must monitor these areas to ensure the child is progressing in each. If there is a deficit, the teacher will implement an intervention and monitor that skill to ensure the child bolsters their understanding. Ultimately, we want children to have automaticity of these skills. This does not mean rapid speed, as is sometimes misunderstood. Automaticity means the skill becomes effortless for the learner. We want these early reading skills to become so effortless that all of their thinking can be used for comprehension and vocabulary. If automaticity of letter names and sounds is not achieved, the child will struggle with reading basic words.

There are five Columns for kindergarten. These Columns allow teachers to use the universal screener to determine if students need assistance with letter names, letter sounds, or both. Further, The Columns allow the teacher to determine if there are deficits in phonological awareness. A final Column exists to monitor which students are on track with sight words.

We devote a chapter to The Columns for first grade because first grade is a year of enormous growth for children. We use the beginning of the first grade year to concentrate on mastering the discreet foundational skills of reading. In the second semester, The Columns data decision rules expand to include oral reading fluency, and will mirror The Columns for grades 2–5.

Can We Use The Columns with Our English Language Learners and Special Education Students?

The Columns are designed for classroom teachers. That said, many of our English language learners and special education students have the same foundational reading needs. Because there are many steps in the processes designed for these learners, we would suggest working with your English learning specialists and your special education departments to see how this best fits into the plans you have for your school.

How Might The Columns Be Helpful for Administrators?

Today's school administrators are expected to be instructional, lead learners. To assist teachers in classrooms and data teams, an administrator must have knowledge in how to identify individual students' academic deficits. When creating The Columns, we found educators using this tool came to us with a wide range of knowledge in foundational reading skills. The Columns provide an easy system for administrators to use with teacher teams. They guide teachers through data analysis, help teachers identify student needs, and ensure that teachers have resources for intervention. Further, due to The Columns' simplistic nature, the administrator does not need to be an expert in reading to use this tool.

Without an understanding by the administrator, building systems of support for students becomes very difficult. As the lead learner, the administrator must know how to identify building needs so budget and professional development resources can be prioritized. Resources, in terms of money and people, must be aligned to the students' needs across all grade levels. The Columns assure an administrator that financial and human capital address the needs of students in the building.

In the chapters ahead, we will explore The Columns in detail. We will discuss the most effective way to utilize The Columns and considerations for implementation. Let's begin by exploring The Columns for kindergarten.

2

Kindergarten and The Columns*

Kindergarten is such a special year. Students are still young and we agree they still need considerable time to explore, investigate, and discover as they are learning. We also believe this is a year that we must closely track their progress in the foundational skills of reading. This doesn't mean teachers should spend hours a day drilling letters and sounds with our 5- and 6-year-old students. However, it does mean that we are intentional with the time we do spend on learning these concepts. Giving students direct, explicit instruction in the components of phonological awareness and phonics is something that should take place each day during the literacy block. "Starting in kindergarten, all children should receive phonological awareness training ... If all children are trained starting in kindergarten, potential reading difficulties can be prevented or minimized" (Kilpatrick, 2016, p. 17).

We also readily admit that there is much more to the reading process that is absolutely necessary. The daily read-alouds, the discussion about story sequence, characters, and other comprehension and vocabulary components are all 100% necessary! Other skills could be listed on The Columns. For the purpose of our tool, we give teachers the ability to hone in on the earliest foundational skills of reading. Our tool provides the teacher with an understanding of where students are in the mastery of those skills. More and more states are requiring school districts to have a dyslexia plan, which requires these early foundational skills to be assessed and monitored. We absolutely agree that mastery of these skills is vital to a child's reading success. The Columns help teachers understand each child's progress toward mastery. For kindergarten, there are five columns. There is always more to think about for kindergarten!

Column 1 in Kindergarten

Students that fall into Column 1 have a strong grasp on phonological awareness along with letter/sound correspondence. Universal screeners completed on these students show they are at or above the 40th percentile in both of these reading components. This means they know their letters, their letter sounds, and that they can hook them together. They have strong alphabetic principle. They also have a strong understanding of phonological awareness. They can rhyme, make substitutions, and segment words. You will likely see these students also doing well in writing because these early foundational skills are so strong. So what do teachers do for these students? Give them more to read! You likely see a spectrum of application among these students. Some are starting to blend words as they read, and others may be reading chapter books. Take some time to divide students in this Column into the needs they have. Group together students that are falling just at the 40th percentile so that they can continue to work on blending their letters and sounds. They should read decodable books so that they can practice applying these skills. Using a site such as Reading A–Z will allow teachers to find decodable books that focus on basic consonant-vowel-consonant (CVC) words. Help students apply the skills they have so that their letter–sound correspondence can continue to grow. Make sure they are transferring these skills to their writing. Help them use their knowledge of sounds to encode when writing stories.

For students who are blending well, give them books with more challenging phonics structures. Use a phonics program that provides systematic, explicit instruction and that follows a scope and sequence. If you are in need of lessons for these advanced phonics skills, one resource might be Sound Partners. These lessons provide systematic, explicit instruction in phonics work that also asks students to apply the decoding in simple sentences, and further asks students to use their skills to apply their knowledge in spelling. These lessons give practice to sight words as well. This simple to use resource provides teachers with a structure to use to teach these advanced kindergarten skills. When searching for a resource for your school, look for a phonics resource that contains a scope and sequence, has explicit lessons, and asks children to decode and encode words.

For students who are already reading, keep moving them forward! They should be concentrating more heavily on comprehension and vocabulary study. They can write about what they are reading and think more deeply about the content they are reading. It's necessary to ensure that these kids are not just reading the words, but rather that they are thinking about meaning. They are still young, and as teachers, we must remember that they may need help comprehending at the level in which they read the words. Asking students to do a basic retell will give you a good idea of how much they understand.

For kids in this column, tracking their mastery of standards is also essential. Through assessment screening, we can see if the foundational skills are mastered, but be sure to concentrate on literary and informational text to ensure they are meeting grade level standards for kindergarten in your state.

In kindergarten, you may see children fall into more than one Column. This is also special and unique to kindergarten, as Columns in grades 1–5 are more distinct. Let's examine Column 2 in kindergarten.

Column 2 in Kindergarten

Students in Column 2 need more practice with letter naming. These students are falling below the 40th percentile on the universal screener. The teacher should analyze the letter naming assessment to gain more information about what is known. In Column 2, you will see a skill checklist listed. This prompts the teacher to determine if errors seem to be random, are typically upper or lower case letters, are letters in the student's name, etc. The teacher should also pay attention to how the student tracks each line. If the student skips lines, it could indicate difficulty tracking text. The teacher should watch for this when doing reading in small groups.

So how does the teacher help students who fall in Column 2? We have found a couple of resources that work well. One of these is Sound Partners, kindergarten edition. This resource was explained in Column 1. Another great resource is a website, www.fcrr.org. This website, created by the Florida Center for Reading Research, has wonderful student center activities. A teacher can locate the K-1 activities and then find the section on phonics. In the phonics section, several activities can be found to assist with letter naming. If a building is doing Wilson Fundations, a double dose of these lessons would also be helpful for students falling in this Column. There are also many Orton-Gillingham-based products that could be used. The intervention for kids in Column 2 should provide direct instruction for letter identification.

Column 3 in Kindergarten

This Column identifies students who need additional practice with letter sounds. These children do not yet have letter sounds mastered, and are falling below the 40th percentile on the universal screener for letter sounds. The teacher should look for patterns in errors. Is the child getting all sounds correct, but slow to say the sound? Are the errors made randomly or is the same letter sound missed each time? Does the student know the letter sounds in their name? The teacher should first determine which students fall in this Column and list names. Once names are listed, the teacher can use the checklist to further divide children into groups that have similar needs, based on the skills checklist in this Column. Once students are identified and placed into groups, the teacher can match an intervention to these needs. Once again, Sound Partners, Fundations, and Orton-Gillingham-based products are all good choices for these students, as is the Florida website (www.fcrr.org). If a teacher uses this website, s/he should look for activities in the K-1 phonics section that concentrate on letter sounds. Direct instruction should be given to students, and it is important that children are not guessing the sound. If a sound is missed, the teacher should correct the sound and ask the child to repeat the sound. Practicing the sound incorrectly will not help the child correct the sound.

Column 4 in Kindergarten

This Column is for students who need additional work in phonological awareness. A universal screener for phonological awareness, such as ISF (initial sound fluency) or PSF (phoneme segmentation fluency), shows if the student is scoring below the 40th percentile. Once students fall into this Column, the teacher needs additional information on what the student does and does not know. In this Column, you will see the various skills included in phonological awareness. In order to know which skills a student has mastered, a teacher needs to give an assessment that identifies skills deficits. One such assessment is the PAST assessment (phonological assessment skills test). At the beginning of kindergarten, it might not be necessary to do this additional assessment on these students. Simply giving students additional instruction in all areas of phonological awareness would be prudent. If at the time the mid-year benchmark is given, and the child is still below the 40th percentile, giving a phonological diagnostic will give the teacher more information about the phonological skills known and not yet mastered by the child. Three resources we have often seen used are the Heggerty Phonemic Awareness curriculum, the Florida website (www.fcrr.org), and the LiPS program by Lindamood-Bell. The Heggerty curriculum provides teachers with simple, easy to use daily lesson plans that span the sequence of phonological skills. If students are far below kindergarten readiness, a preschool curriculum is available. We have found the preschool curriculum to be useful as an intervention for students not quite kindergarten-ready. The Heggerty curriculum for kindergarten is a great

Tier 1 resource for daily work in the area of phonological awareness, and for kids falling in this Column, they simply receive an additional dose of time with these lessons.

If the Florida Center website is used, teachers should locate the K-1 center activities and then the phonological awareness component. The teacher will find several activities listed by the skills checklist found in Column 4. There is also a tab for preschool, called VPK Learning Center Activities. For students that have had little exposure to phonological awareness, these activities might be appropriate.

The Lindamood-Bell program is a robust program that can be used in both Tier 1 and for intervention.

Columns Case # 1
Kindergarten
Column placement: Columns 2, 3, and 4

Student: Sophia
Data: Letter naming fluency: 31st percentile
Letter sound fluency: 28th percentile
Phoneme segmentation fluency: 18th percentile
Phonological awareness diagnostic: Concerns with onset/rime, initial sounds as a start
Phonics survey: Letter ID: Need b, d, p, q, m, n; letter sounds: all vowels
District high frequency word assessment: No concerns

Instructional focus: Universal screening tools indicate that Sophia is low in automaticity of letter naming, letter sound, and phoneme segmentation. Specific needs are further identified. Sophia is placed in Columns 2, 3, and 4 after analyzing her data. She has knowledge of most letters, but does not know them fluently. A 30-minute intervention is scheduled where Sophia will work on letter name and letter sounds. During Tier 1 small group, Sophia will receive additional support with phonological awareness, beginning with onset/rime.

Materials: Sophia's teacher will use Wilson Fundations. Sophia's teachers will access FCRR and district materials for all other activities.

Column 5 in Kindergarten

This Column is for students who need additional practice with high frequency words. These children need to work on saying them, and most likely, spelling them. The teacher should use a high frequency word assessment that gives information about what words the student knows. It may be that teachers do not begin this assessment until mid-year. Giving students the first semester to work with these words will give them time to practice and know the words that are expected. Researchers offer suggestions on how teachers might teach high frequency words (e.g., Ayala & O'Connor, 2013; January, Lovelace, Foster, & Ardoin, 2017).

1. Introduce new sight words in isolation (i.e., the sight word by itself), but immediately follow this with repeated exposures to the same sight words in books and other text materials.
2. Do not introduce two sight words that are similar or easily confused at the same time. For instance, "will" and "well" should be introduced in separate lessons as should "on" and "no."
3. Provide brief (i.e., less than 10 minutes per session) but frequent sight word instruction, especially for beginning and struggling readers.
4. Offer students numerous opportunities to practice and receive immediate, specific feedback. For example, if a child reads the word "this" correctly, respond with positive feedback: "Yes! The word is *this*." If a child read "this" incorrectly, respond with corrective feedback: "The word is *this*. Say the word *this*."

The Iowa Center for Reading Research gives great tips for this and many other components of reading (https://iowareadingresearch.org/blog/teaching-sight-words).

In this chapter, we have reviewed each Column for kindergarten. Teachers should complete the assessment screening period and use the data collected to determine where students fall in each foundational skill for reading. Using The Columns will allow teachers to determine the focus for students, thus giving the teacher the ability to hone in on the missing skills and help children close the gap for the identified foundational reading deficit. In a later chapter, we will see kindergarten mock data that will allow teachers to practice moving students into Columns to identify foundational reading need and then match the intervention.

Frequently Asked Questions for Kindergarten

- ♦ What if some of my students fall in multiple columns?
  - This is common in kindergarten. Some students come to us with little background in foundational reading skills. This is

why it is so important to have a solid Tier 1 resource for teaching these skills. All students in kindergarten should receive explicit, systematic instruction that follows a scope and sequence in phonological awareness and phonics. Create groups once all kids are placed in Columns. You will see that some kids are in multiple columns and they can be placed together.

- **Do I need to start intervention at the beginning of the year in kindergarten?**
  - This is something that should be considered at the school level, and often on a case-by-case basis. There is merit in allowing kindergarten students to take the first semester to gain exposure to these skills. That said, this is assuming there are quality Tier 1 resources in place, and teachers are still watching students by progress monitoring throughout the first semester. If students are not making gains naturally by October, the teacher should consider giving extra, targeted practice to students. The earlier we intervene, the easier it is to close gaps for students.

- **Do kindergarten students really need explicit, systematic instruction?**
  - Yes! We absolutely believe this is necessary. This does not mean other parts of the day can't be exploratory. It just means that for a part of the day, students should receive explicit, systematic instruction in phonics and phonological awareness.

- **My school takes a balanced literacy approach to reading. How do The Columns help me?**
  - It is likely that you use an assessment to gauge what students know and don't know when it comes to foundational reading skills. Using an assessment that is nationally normed, reliable, and valid ensures your expectations are in line with what kids should know. This assessment will give you a percentile that can then be used to help guide The Columns analysis.

- **I assess my students for more areas of reading than is listed in The Columns, such as oral language/vocabulary. Why isn't it listed?**

  – There are other factors that influence literacy that are not in The Columns. Our intent was to keep The Columns concise and focused on some key essential student needs in learning to read.

- **Why do we time students when they do early literacy assessments?**

  – Automaticity of the skill is important. It's not about speed, it's about ensuring the child knows the letters and sounds to automaticity. We often say to a teacher, if the child knows the letter A, they will know it anywhere – on an alphabet chart, in a book, on a whiteboard, on a street sign, etc. They have automaticity of the letter without having to take time to study it first. We want children to have automaticity of letter names and sounds so that this is not something they need to think about. We are not trying to get children to beat the timer, we are trying to ensure they know letters and letter sounds without great effort.

Note

* To review The Columns for kindergarten, see pages 4–5.

3

Grade 1 and The Columns*

First grade is a time for vast growth. As we work with teacher teams, we witness the first-grade student's journey from possessing basic foundational skills to gaining fluency in text. Kindergarten has built a base. Now we are reinforcing and building on those skills to begin to dive further into text. Because of this transition, we devote a chapter to The Columns in first grade. There are two sets of Columns for this grade level. One is for the first semester and another for the second semester, when the expectation of gaining fluency in text is added. Because of the intricacies at this time, the number of Columns is expanded to six in first semester and then reduced to four in second semester. By doing this, we are able to further distinguish the needs for first grade as reading skills develop throughout the year.

First Grade, First Semester: Column 1 – High Phonological/Phonemic Awareness, High Phonics

Prior to first grade, students have been building skills in letter identification, letter sound acquisition, phonological skills, and sight words. First grade continues to add to this. Some students will be advanced in this skill sequence, and others will need additional support. The Columns for first grade, first semester, represent the range of student ability and student need.

For students in Column 1, we begin to see the processes of reading come together. Phonological awareness is essential, from beginning rhyming and syllable segmenting to advanced phonemic awareness. Phoneme blending and segmenting are key for first-grade students. Students in

Column 1 can accurately apply these concepts in multiple situations. They show their knowledge on universal screening tools. For example, these students fall at the 40th percentile and above on tests such as phoneme segmentation fluency.

Column 1 also references knowledge of phonics, in which students in this column are proficient. They have knowledge of letter identification, letter sound, and consonant-vowel-consonant combinations. On universal screeners, students again fall above the 40th percentile on subtests related to phonics, such as nonsense word fluency. Although a phonics survey is not required for Column 1, teachers may choose to utilize one to find a more complex instructional focus. When given the phonics survey, these students may demonstrate mastery farther into the skill sequence than what is currently being instructed in Tier 1 whole group. Students may be at grade level or they may be more advanced in their understanding of phonics.

Time should be allotted for students in Column 1 to read, to apply skills they have learned to text. Students may be able to accurately identify letters, sounds, or elements of phonics, but utilizing those pieces of knowledge simultaneously when reading can be more difficult. Selection of text should mirror student need, which for Column 1 may be far more complex than grade level.

Comprehension is the goal of reading. Students at the lowest grade levels are provided guidance in monitoring comprehension, literal comprehension, and retell, for example. State standards relay what should be instructed within first grade, including concepts related to characters, setting, and plot. Students in Column 1 experience extra support in prioritized comprehension strategies and skills based on these standards.

First Grade, First Semester: Columns 2–6 Overview

What differentiates Columns 2–6 for first grade, first semester is the extent of the strengths and insufficiencies within the scope and sequence of both phonemic awareness and phonics. The Columns are structured in this manner to help design intervention to match the needs of the learner. Below you will find the outline of Columns 2–6. Column 2 is the only column that meets benchmark scores on phonological assessments. Note the differences in the percentile ranges for phonics.

Column 2: High in phonological/phonemic awareness, phonics low
Column 3: Low in phonological/phonemic awareness, phonics high

Column 4: Low in phonological/phonemic awareness, phonics scoring at the 25th–39th percentiles

Column 5: Low in phonological/phonemic awareness, phonics scoring at the 11th–24th percentiles

Column 6: Low in phonological/phonemic awareness, phonics scoring below the 10th percentile

First Grade, First Semester: Columns 2–6 – A Range in Phonological/Phonemic Awareness Ability

Column 2 begins much the same as Column 1 in that students master phonological skills. Scores on universal screeners related to this area are above the 40th percentile. Specifically, students are able to complete phoneme blending and segmenting activities with accuracy.

As we venture into Columns 3–6 first grade, first semester, be sure to note that all of these columns are low in phonological/phonemic awareness skills. The phonological awareness universal screener falls below the 40th percentile. The phonological awareness diagnostic should be administered to help gain perspective on which skills to address during intervention. The difference between The Columns will be the severity of the need within the phonological awareness scope and sequence. Column 3 will fall just below benchmark scores, which indicates students needing support with the latter phonological skills, such as phoneme blending and segmenting. By Column 6, students may struggle with beginning ideas such as concept of word, syllable segmenting, and onset/rime.

Through many years, we worked with countless first grade teacher teams to analyze data and determine the correct course of instruction. During these meetings, teams would discuss the difficulty of some first grade students to blend: "phoneme blending, is one of the most important and surprisingly, difficult jobs for the beginning reader to master" (Shaywitz, 2005, p. 184). Discussions about blending would start in relation to phonics. For example, a student may come to the word "cat" while reading and pronounce it "tac" or something entirely different. Think about the processes a student must execute to get the end result of "cat." They must be able to identify the letters in the word, hook that letter to a sound, and use phonological skills to map the sounds into a word. If there is a deficit in any of these areas, the student will struggle. At times it may not be with smaller consonant-vowel-consonant words, but could be experienced as words become more complex. For these students, administer the phonological awareness survey. We find that some students will pass easily and should continue to practice blending in text.

However, with students that have significant holes in their phonological diagnostic results, the intervention should have a concentration of time on phonemic awareness skills, particularly phoneme blending. The student that couldn't get the letter, letter sound, and phonological concepts to come together to make "cat," may need to go back to practice without the text in phoneme blending activities. If they get better with these activities, you should see an increase in the ability to blend in text.

Look to your district for intervention materials in phonemic awareness. Suggestions are listed in The Columns. Marilyn Jager Adams' *Phonemic Awareness in Young Children* and David Kilpatrick's *Equipped for Reading Success* are two resources that support phonological development.

Columns Case #2
First grade, first semester
Column placement: Column 4

Student: Rockus
Data: Universal screener composite: Below 40th percentile
        Nonsense word fluency: 28th percentile
        Phoneme segmentation fluency: Below 40th percentile
        Phonological awareness diagnostic: Multiple concerns
        Phonics survey: Letter ID correct, missing vowel sounds, multiple errors on initial and final sounds in consonant-vowel-consonant combinations
        District high frequency word assessment: Knows 26 of first 45 words

Instructional focus: Universal screeners are low. A 30-minute intervention time is allocated for phonological awareness and phonics needs, including missing vowel sounds and CVC combinations. An additional 15 minutes of phonological awareness instruction is provided by a Title 1 or special reading teacher, starting with the first need found within the scope and sequence of skills. Tier 1 small group focuses on reading text that helps support CVC combinations. Identified sight words, vowel sounds, and CVC combinations are reinforced during literacy station times. A listening station provides a model for fluid reading of text.

Materials: Rockus's teacher will use 95 Percent group phonics and phonemic awareness intervention materials. Rockus's teachers will access FCRR and district materials for all other activities.

First Grade, First Semester: Columns 2–6 – A Range in Phonics Ability

Let's begin with Column 2. As mentioned above, these students are proficient in phonological skills. Areas of deficit are phonics related. Students in this Column score below the 40th percentile on a phonics universal screener. Phonics will, therefore, be the instructional focus for this group of children. A phonics survey is administered to pinpoint the instructional focus. To help transition students from practicing skills to applying skills in text, teachers should utilize connected text.

Column 3 is the opposite of Column 2. Students in this Column are able to master phonics skills, so they are considered at grade level at least. They have proven this through the universal screener score surpassing the 40th percentile. Phonological and phonemic awareness skills are not at grade level. This is the main area of intervention for these students as mentioned above.

For the students in Columns 4–6, teacher teams deliberate the many obstacles that become a factor in learning to read. Phonological/phonemic awareness scores are low. In Columns 5 and 6, there are significantly more skills that are not mastered compared with the students in Column 4. The same can be said for phonics. Students falling in Column 4 do struggle, but students in Columns 5 and 6 are even farther back in the phonological and phonics skill sequences. Performance on the phonics survey or the phonological awareness diagnostic will show greater deficits. A more intensive intervention will be required. Intensity can be increased by the frequency of the intervention, including number of days per week. It can also be increased through the length of the lesson and the number of students in the group. Column 6 represents the students with the greatest insufficiencies. Compared to all groups, the intensity of the intervention would be the greatest for these students. The smallest groups, the greatest frequency, the longest lessons, and the depth of the intervention are the hallmark of Column 6. Specific interventions are listed for phonics in the columns. As we have already mentioned earlier, we do not promote any one program over another. However, Wilson Fundations is one resource that provides support for phonics, phonological understanding, and letter formation. It can be used in all tiers of intervention for first grade students.

To develop organized plans of instruction for Column 4–6 students, we have found that meeting in teacher teams can be effective. A team meeting may include grade level teachers, EL teachers, reading teachers, special education teachers, and administrators. The list of student needs may be too long to fit into one intervention time. At team meetings, decisions regarding which teacher will be addressing which needs during the day, throughout the week can be coordinated. For example, phonics and phonological skill intervention may be implemented during an RTI time. Reading with connected text for those same skills may occur during Tier 1 small group. Additional sight word support may be a piece included by a reading teacher. Because there are a number of deficient areas, the greatest need would be scheduled during the most intensive time, but other needs could be reinforced at other times of the day. Time to meet as a teacher team to review data and plan instruction is crucial in this coordinated effort.

First Grade, Second Semester

One joy of first grade is to witness students being able to tap into their knowledge of reading in order to decode print and comprehend new books they are discovering. The second semester denotes a continuing change for first grade students. They pour into text gaining fluency of words and phrases, resulting in an overall fluency of reading. One way to measure a student's ability to read fluently is to check a word per minute rate. Universal screeners are available to help with this, including oral reading fluency which is just one example of the many available. Students read for 1 minute to achieve a benchmark or progress monitoring score. The Columns for the second semester include a fluency score as part of the data at the top of each column. This is in contrast to The Columns for first grade, first semester.

First Grade, Second Semester: Column 1 – Meets or Exceeds Fluency Benchmark Scores

Students in Column 1, first grade, second semester, will perform at or above expectation on a fluency measure such as oral reading fluency. This includes meeting the 40th percentile or exceeding that mark. These students have mastered phonics and phonemic awareness skills in the past and are able to apply those skills to text. Enrichment for these students includes much of what was written for the first semester. An addition is the continued improvement of fluency as text becomes more complex through the year.

First Grade, Second Semester: Column 2

Students in Column 2 fall just below benchmark goals, scoring at the 25th–39th percentiles in oral reading fluency. There may be varying reasons for this shortfall. To decide if there is an underlying problem that is keeping the students from achieving the fluency goal, the teacher should administer the phonics survey. If a need for phonics is found after giving the survey, these students will move to Column 3 which addresses additional phonics support. The phonological awareness diagnostic should also be administered. We do this because teachers should rule out a deficit in phonological awareness for the student to remain in Column 2.

Students who are listed in Column 2, therefore, are not found to have any outside phonics or phonological awareness problems. They are able to perform skills up through Tier 1 phonics instruction. The area of deficit is being able to fluently use those skills while reading. Intervention should be targeted here. Additional interventions may be added to Column 2 by your district. Interventions can include practice of word fluency, phrases, and passage fluency.

Columns Case #3
First grade, second semester
Column placement: Column 2

Student: Alejandra
Data: Universal screener composite: 34th percentile
        Oral reading fluency: 27th percentile
        Phonological awareness diagnostic: No concerns
        Phonics survey: No concerns
        Notes on comprehension: Can do basic retell

Instructional focus: Alejandra is slightly below benchmark goals in oral reading. She has no underlying phonological or phonics concerns, so an emphasis for intervention should be placed on becoming more fluent with text. This does not mean reading as fast as possible, but improving the automaticity at which words are read. A 30-minute intervention time is allocated for the improvement of fluency. During Tier 1 small group, comprehension and fluency of text will be reinforced.

Materials: Alejandra's teachers will access FCRR and district materials for all other activities.

First Grade, Second Semester: Columns 3 and 4

Fluency is again the universal screening score used as the initial consideration for finding students that fall into Column 3. Students in this Column fall between the 11th and 24th percentiles on the universal screener. Column 4 student scores are lower, falling below the 10th percentile. Students in Column 4 are significantly below the universal screening goal. Students in Columns 3 and 4 should be given the phonics survey and the phonological awareness diagnostic. Students in Column 3 may or may not have a phonological deficit. Column 4 students will likely have this need. Both Column 3 and 4 students will need to work on an aspect of the phonics scope and sequence. Students in Column 4 may be working on letter identification or letter sound, while students in Column 3 may be farther up the skill sequence, improving use of consonant blends, for example. The instructional focus for each group is dependent on the information found in the phonics survey and should be matched to the intervention. A goal is to master the phonics and any phonological awareness need, which in turn will support becoming a more fluent reader.

Frequently Asked Questions for First Grade

- **In kindergarten, there is a Column for high frequency words. Where is that for first grade?**

  - We do believe the teacher should continue to monitor high frequency words in first grade. We left if out of The Columns for grade levels past kindergarten because it becomes too much information to keep in The Columns. First grade is particularly complex. For Columns work, we wanted to keep the teacher attuned to the foundational skills necessary for a child to become a fluent reader. We do think the teacher should continue to monitor the mastery of high frequency words for all students.

- **The first semester of first grade seems really complicated. Is there a way to make it simpler?**

  - First grade is complex! Teachers are expected to ensure students have mastered the foundational skills for reading and apply those skills in books. It is a huge year of growth for students. We have found that it is useful for teachers to concentrate on closely monitoring the foundational skills in the first semester and then concentrate on moving students toward fluency in the second semester. Of course, you will have some students reading from the moment they walk into your first grade classroom. How wonderful! These students fall in Column 1 and will begin working on or above grade level to continue their growth forward.

- **I don't see a composite score for each Column in first grade. Why do I only see it in Column 1?**
  - In order to ensure the teacher is finding the deficit foundational reading skills in first grade, we feel it is necessary to have a screener that assesses for phonological and phonics skills. If your screener gives you a composite score, look for the areas within that tell you more about how your student did on the phonological and phonics components of the screener. If you do not get a score in these components, you will need to rely on the information you learn through the phonics survey and phonological awareness diagnostic.

Note

* To review The Columns for first grade, see pages 6–10.

4

Column 1 for Grades 2–5[*]
A Focus on Comprehension and Standards

Comprehension is the ultimate goal of the reading process. Therefore, we monitor student progress toward proficient use of comprehension strategies and skills. As teachers, we wish for our students to not only understand how to use these skills and strategies with the text we read together, but to also be able to apply them to texts read independently as well. We hope students will be able to utilize abilities in comprehension with a variety of genres, including narrative, informational, and opinion-based text. As educators, we support comprehension work in Tier 1 whole group, Tier 1 small group, and intervention/enrichment settings. In reviewing student needs in comprehension, Column 1 is divided into two sections. Both sections focus on comprehension, but are separated by a student's proficiency with standards.

The Top of Column 1 for Grades 2–5

At the very beginning of the school year, elementary students are screened for essential reading components, including comprehension, vocabulary, fluency, phonics, and phonological awareness. Screeners detect overall performance of the student, but also help to pinpoint need. It is important to note which skills the universal screener is targeting. Some will address fluency, phonics, or phonemic awareness. General comprehension of a passage may also be assessed, such as literal comprehension or retell. Additionally, some universal screeners are now including vocabulary.

Students in the top section of Column 1 meet benchmark scores as designated on screening assessments. These students are performing as expected or higher on district and classroom assessments. They are proficient in the reading components of phonics and phonological awareness. They are able to assimilate those skills into fluent reading. Fluency rate of reading scores are on or above what is expected. Students at the top of Column 1 also meet basic comprehension criteria as deemed by the universal screening assessment. Their scores are grade level or higher on comprehension assessments. They are able to master literal comprehension, monitoring comprehension, or basic retell. Overall performance on the universal screener is above the 40th percentile.

The purpose of The Columns is to help identify the next need of the student and hook that need to instruction and/or intervention. Even though students at the top of Column 1 are proficient, an instructional focus for these students should still be identified. A focus on state standards can help provide a framework for identifying what is next. In addition, school districts should utilize a consistent method to deem what is proficient in relation to state standards. Common formative assessments (Ainsworth & Viegut, 2006) can be built by staff within school districts. Purchased systems now exist that help with assessment of standards, such as iReady, Evaluate, Mastery Connect, Galileo, etc. Whether purchased or created in-house, districts should evaluate whether the method of common formative assessment that is utilized in schools matches the expectation and language of their own state's standards, so that there is alignment between the standard and the common formative assessment. For example, students may be asked to write summaries in class by their teacher, but the standard and state assessment will ask them to evaluate multiple summaries to decide which best fits a passage. Students may perform poorly at state level because the district practices do not align with state expectations. Common formative assessments in comprehension generally focus on skills such as main idea, point of view, author's purpose, narrative analysis, theme, compare/contrast, etc. Teachers may also choose to assess comprehension strategies such as schema, determining importance, and visualizing during the course of classroom instruction. Student response and structured conversations will provide insight into the daily application of these strategies (Harvey & Goudvis, 2017, p. 67).

Instruction for Students at the Top of Column 1

For students at the top of Column 1, the Tier 1 curriculum is a focus for instruction. One to three comprehension standards may be identified as needing improvement. Students may study grade level expectations for that standard, or they can move up the progression of skills related to that standard. What is the expectation of the standard at this grade level? How does the expectation for the standard increase as it moves to the next grade level? What elements of the standard change? Students may be working to master the standard at their own grade level, or may be working on the progression of the standard as it moves forward. Teachers should have information available on how that standard links to academic language, learning goals, and district instructional tools. Simple documents can be created specific to district assessment and instructional materials that help build this path for teachers. This will help to ensure that the expectations of the standards make it to instruction in the classroom.

We wish for students to experience texts in a variety of formats. Books, articles, and other print material are a start. Digital reading can encompass research and various comprehension standards. A variety of reading sites will help to serve as a resource for teachers including Newsela and CommonLit. Students may also be able to work on listening skills and standards through audio resources. Comprehension skills can be applied as students listen to text.

Columns Case #4
Grades 2–5
Column placement: The top of Column 1

Student: Maggie
Grade: 5
Data: Universal screener composite: 87th percentile
          Most recent state testing: Advanced
          Common formative assessments: All at 90% or above

Instructional focus: Maggie's teacher decided, due to analysis of district data, to focus on state standards related to claims, evidence, and reasoning for students falling at the top of Column 1. The state requires students to apply these concepts in reading, in writing opinion pieces, and in listening activities. Maggie's teacher is going to have students not only know these fifth grade concepts, but also design instruction so students collaboratively and independently apply these to text. She will advance some students into concepts found in sixth grade claims, evidence, and reasoning standards and again have them apply knowledge in a variety of ways during reading, writing, and speaking/listening activities.

Materials: Maggie's teacher will utilize district materials that support these standards.

Students in the Lower Section of Column 1

Students at the lower section of Column 1 have also mastered decoding and fluency of reading words. They are able to demonstrate phonological awareness, phonics, and fluency skills. Given an oral rate of reading assessment, these students are proven to meet fluency benchmarks. The distinction between the top of Column 1 and the bottom of Column 1 is the ability to use basic comprehension skills. The bottom of Column 1 focuses on students that struggle with basic comprehension. For example, they may be unable to monitor comprehension, answer literal comprehension questions, or provide a simple retell. In other words, they may sound perfect when reading aloud, but can't explain what they have read. They may not be able to tell the most basic information about characters in a story or the main ideas of an informational text. These students have low comprehension assessment scores on universal screeners. Because of this struggle, they are also unable to perform well on the reading strategies and skills measured through the standards work. Overall, fluency and phonics are high, comprehension scores are low.

Intervening with Students in the Lower Section of Column 1

Students in the lower section of Column 1 need more than just standards work. They need help with the simplest forms of comprehension, as well as additional support in developing their vocabulary. Intervention for this group may occur in small group, RTI, or at other times of the day. They should receive an intervention in this area of literacy just as there are interventions in fluency, phonics, or phonological awareness. There are various research-based programs available. One example is the PALS program through Vanderbilt University. Other resources we have seen used across tiers of instruction include Making Meaning and the Comprehension Toolkit by Stephanie Harvey and Anne Goudvis. Assessment systems like iReady come with intervention materials matched to student need. In addition to this, there are many web-based programs that provide practice opportunities for certain comprehension standards. Some we have seen used are Freckle, EdCite, Commonlit, and Newsela. Match what you have in your school to students who fall in this lower level of Column 1 to ensure these students are given the tools they need to increase their understanding of what is read.

> Columns Case #5
> Grades 2–5
> Column placement: The bottom of Column 1
>
> Student: Domionte
> Grade: 4
> Data: Universal screener composite: 52nd percentile
>   Oral reading fluency: 74th percentile
>   Most recent state testing: Basic (not to proficient)
>   Common formative assessments: Scores around 70% on comprehension CFAs
>
> Instructional focus: The composite score and the oral reading score support Domionte's ability to utilize phonological awareness, phonics, and fluency skills well. He is secure in being able to fluently read grade level text. Scores from state testing and common formative assessments point to comprehension as the instructional focus, but we still need to get more specific. Comprehension is too broad. For students like Domionte at the bottom of Column 1, it is best to also check basic comprehension skills, such as literal comprehension, monitoring comprehension, and retell. In further assessment, Domionte is unable to answer literal comprehension questions or questions with information directly stated in the text. Support with literal comprehension is the next instructional focus for Domionte.
>
> Materials: Domionte's teachers will utilize district materials that support these standards.

One Extra Caveat for Fourth and Fifth Grades

Students in fourth and fifth grade have, in most cases, already participated in state assessment. According to state exam scores, they may be designated as below basic, basic, proficient, or advanced in relation to state assessment. Particular sessions focus on literature and informational comprehension standards. When considering whether students are placed in the upper or lower section of Column 1, the state assessment provides another piece of information regarding how a student can perform in relation to standards. If students consistently perform basic or below basic on standard assessment, then students should be placed at the bottom of Column 1.

Frequently Asked Questions for Column 1 in Grades 2–5

- **What if my students at the top of Column 1 have already mastered grade level comprehension standards?**
    - Comprehension standards are the first goal for students at the top of Column 1. If mastery of these standards has occurred, then

additional literacy standards may be taken into further consideration. There is a range of understanding within the group at the top of Column 1. Some may be very proficient with comprehension skills and strategies. They are able to take standards through a learning progression to higher grade levels. The next step is to look at other literacy standards. Writing, research, and speaking and listening standards may be the next focus for instruction for students in this Column. Common formative assessments for these standards can be identified by the district. Identify the two or three standards for improvement based on data. Instructional time can focus on these standards.

- ◆ **What if the student is almost meeting the 40th percentile, but not quite? Do I leave that student out of Column 1?**

    – Screening tools will designate a percentile score for the student. Teachers will sometimes ask about students that are just below the designated percentile. For example, a student scores at the 37th percentile on the overall composite score, but scores at the 68th percentile on a word per rate fluency measure. The student is above expectation in fluency and decoding. They should move into the bottom of Column 1 because the student's need is comprehension, even if the overall composite score is just below the 40th percentile cut-off for Column 1.

- ◆ **Can a student that is placed at the top of Column 1 score basic on the state test?**

    – This is always possible. When you see this, the teacher should ask additional questions. Does the student rush through work? What is the motivation level? Is there testing anxiety? Is the student missing deeper understanding of the state standards? Finding a student that does well on everything except the state test should prompt the teacher to look into the reasons behind this.

- ◆ **Are there extra ways to practice my state's standards?**

    – There are many online sites that now offer state standards support. EdCite, Freckle, Commonlit, Newsela, etc., all allow a teacher to assign standards to students, based on those standards that students might need additional support to master. Determine what your school has to offer to students for standards work.

- **What about vocabulary?**
    - Depending on the universal screener that you use, you may or may not receive a score for vocabulary. If your tool does provide a percentile, use that to tell you how the students are doing in this reading component. If your tool does not provide a percentile, it is fairly safe to assume that vocabulary instruction is an ongoing need for all students. There are many books that dive deeply into how to consider teaching vocabulary to students. One researcher we have relied on over the years is Isabel Beck. Through her work in *Bringing Words to Life*, Beck examines which words to select, how well students know words, and the type of instruction that research shows to be the most effective (Beck, 2013).

- **My universal screener provides a composite percentage and there are percentages for individual reading components. Which one do I use to initially place kids in The Columns?**
    - First use the composite score to begin thinking about where to place the student. For kids in Column 1, you would then look at the other scores that make up the composite to make sure none stand out as a deficit for the student. For example, the composite may be high, but you see that the fluency score is low. The teacher will need to know if fluency is impacting the student's ability to learn. It could be that they just process more slowly, but this is not blocking the ability to comprehend at high levels. If this is the case, we would not be overly concerned with a slightly lower fluency score for a student falling in Column 1. Only when fluency is a barrier to comprehension does it become a concern. You might also see students become frustrated or anxious because it takes them longer to do a task. In contrast, you might see that the composite is high, but the vocabulary score is low. This is something to target for students, as vocabulary can directly impact comprehension as students progress through the grade levels.

Note

* To review The Columns for Grades 2–5, see pages 11–12.

5
Column 2 for Grades 2–5*

The Importance of Fluency in the Reading Process

Students who decode fluently can focus on comprehension of text. When we learn a particular skill, and practice it over a period of time, we eventually demonstrate the skill without needing to concentrate on every aspect of performing the task. Playing an instrument, making a free throw in basketball, or driving a car all becomes easier with additional practice. Reading is the same in that we develop automaticity of skill. Automaticity refers to how effortlessly we can access and perform skills in the process of being fluent. Students who can decode fluently have become very efficient at foundational reading skills, and they easily read words, thus freeing their mind to concentrate on comprehension of the text at hand. We have mentioned automaticity in earlier chapters, but the concept very much pertains here. It is not about speed and getting students to read really fast, but about students being effortless in reading phrases in a text. We want students to be able to think about what they are reading and gain meaning – that is the goal. Timothy Rasinski states, "Word recognition automaticity is the ability of readers to decode words with so little cognitive effort that they can direct those cognitive energies to comprehension" (2017, p. 520). John Hattie further reinforces this idea (2009, p. 135), "the skills of automaticity in word recognition and decoding (the move from accurate to automatic word reading) need to be specifically assessed and taught."

Fluency plays an important role in the process of learning to read in grades 2 through 5. Fluency encompasses various elements, including rate, expression, and prosody. Prosody includes the phrasing, tone, and pitch at which reading occurs. Deficits in these skills can cause reading to be staggered, lack phrasing, and become labored. We have assessed and instructed students whose phrasing while reading was one word at a time. Other students may have had longer phrasing, but still had to concentrate on the decoding process, slowing comprehension. Providing intervention in the component of fluency helps a student to work on all of these skills.

Column 2 for Grades 2–5

"Tests of reading fluency represent an important piece of information that can assist evaluators in gaining better understanding of a student's reading skill" (Kilpatrick, 2015, p. 219). Rate of reading is one indicator.

To measure rate of reading, the number of words a student reads per minute can be used as an indicator. The rate per minute can indicate how automatically the student is able to decode. Norms for a grade level rate of reading are set by assessing hundreds of students (Hasbrouck & Tindal, 2006). When students are reading, we know they will slow down, or read more quickly, depending on content, prior knowledge and understanding, along with efficiency of decoding. Students must learn to adjust reading rate for better comprehension.

Column 2 focuses on the need for students to read fluently. The first piece of data used to identify students for this Column is the percentile scored on the universal screener. Students in Column 2 are below the 40th percentile in reading. This is generally determined through the use of an oral reading fluency rate, or an overall composite score.

Students in this Column are reading below the 40th percentile according to the universal screener. Some students may score just under the norm. They may be reading in longer phrases and just need some additional strategies to help them maintain fluency goals. Other students may be farther from the norm. In this case, we need to consider if there might be underlying issues that are keeping the student from obtaining proficiency in fluency. To determine this, the teacher must take the next step listed in Column 2, deciding if the student truly has a deficit in fluency, or if the deficit in fluency is masked by an actual deficit in phonics.

Distinguishing Phonics and Fluency Needs

Students who fall below the 40th percentile may have skill deficits in phonics. We screen students for these phonics deficits when we see a low fluency rate of reading. In other words, if students are reading more slowly than expected, is it because they are not able to decode words efficiently and are they struggling to do so? Some students will be able to figure out a word, but this may require them to break it apart first and blend it back together. If they do this multiple times throughout a text, rate of reading drops. The student's ability to decode is present, but they may not be able to do it with efficiency, thus indicating a deficit in the automaticity of phonics skills. You may also see a student that has memorized many words and might appear fluent. However, when faced with a word they do not know, they lack the decoding skills necessary to attack the word.

A universal screener that provides a word per minute rate may also produce an accuracy score. The accuracy score is an indicator of decoding or phonics needs. The accuracy score is configured by subtracting the number of errors (words missed) from the total number of words. That number will then be divided by the total number of words, producing an accuracy score. For example, if there are 250 words and the student misses 34 of them, you would subtract 34 from 250, which equals 216. You would then divide 216 by 250 and multiply by 100 to get 86%, which would be the accuracy score for that particular reading. We would hope for students to be able to read with an accuracy score above 95% so that the student does not have to concentrate on decoding, and can concentrate on comprehension of the passage.

The word systematic is often mentioned when talking about phonics. It refers to the scope and sequence of skills from easiest to hardest. The scope and sequence may begin with letter identification and letter sounds, and then progress into consonant-vowel-consonant words (cat, dog), consonant blends and digraphs (stop, shut), vowel team and vowel r combinations, multisyllabic words, and so forth. Students may easily decode earlier aspects of this sequence, yet struggle with higher level skills. This struggle with certain aspects of the sequence can hinder overall fluency and produce a low word per minute rate.

The teacher must determine if students that fall in Column 2 truly have a fluency need. To do this, Column 2 suggests giving a phonics survey to rule out a phonics concern. Examples of these tools include, but are not limited to, the Really Great Reading Company's Decoding Survey, Jan Hasbrouck's Quick Phonics Screener, and the 95 Percent Group PSI Phonics Screener. Students are asked to read real words or nonsense words for each level of phonics skill. If phonics skills are found to be deficient for students in Column 2, we draw the conclusion that students should not remain in Column 2. In this case, these students would be moved to Column 3.

Students in Column 2 have fluency needs, but do not have a deficit in phonics. These students have mastered phonics skills, but are unable to apply them with efficient automaticity, therefore producing a low word per minute rate. As a next step in this Column, teachers will recommend placing Column 2 students into a fluency intervention.

Columns Case #6
Grades 2–5
Column placement: Column 2

Student: Hilario
Grade: 3
Data: Universal screener composite: 42nd percentile
        Oral reading fluency: 31st percentile
        Phonics survey: No phonics concerns
        Phonological awareness diagnostic: No concerns
        Most recent state testing: Not yet taken
        Common formative assessments: Scores around 75% on comprehension CFAs

Instructional focus: The composite score is barely over the benchmark (Column 1), but oral reading is below (Column 2). No significant phonics or phonological awareness concerns were found. Since phonics skill development is not an underlying issue, Hilario will be placed in Column 2. The instructional focus for his 30-minute intervention time will be fluency development. Improvement in this area may likely also advance comprehension, another area of concern. Tier 1 small group instruction will focus on comprehension, particularly text evidence and inference, an area found to be in greatest need through common formative assessments.

Materials: Read Naturally will be used during intervention time to support fluency development. Hilario's teachers will utilize district materials to support comprehension work.

Hooking Assessment Information to Intervention

Students need to have direct, explicit instruction in the area of fluency if listed in Column 2. Fluency needs can vary. Fluency issues can be related to rate, phrasing, rereading, self correction, or expression, for example. Teachers should look for patterns of behavior. A main goal is for the information found in analysis through The Columns to directly impact the intervention that will take place.

Different programs for intervention exist for fluency. There are well-researched strategies and programs that exist for instruction of students performing just below the norm for rate of reading. Read Naturally is a program we have seen used in many districts. There are many choices for research-based fluency programs for schools to examine, and there are many great books written on this reading component that offer wonderful strategies for increasing a student's fluency skills. The name of fluency intervention(s) in your district should be identified and listed in Column 2.

Frequently Asked Questions about Column 2

- **We have tried using a fluency program, but we aren't seeing the results we anticipated. Any suggestions?**
    - Make sure you are taking the extra step to rule out phonics, as discussed above. A student may appear to have a fluency need, but if there are underlying phonics concerns, the teacher must know that. To do this, give the phonics survey to ensure there are no missing skills. Also, implementation is key to intervention success. If the fluency word per minute rate does not increase, then implementation and fidelity of the intervention should be considered. Is the intervention being implemented as stated within the guidelines of the program? In other words, is it being altered in a way that is making it less successful? The time allotted for an intervention is also a consideration. The amount of time per day and number of times per week that students experience the intervention should be calculated. Is the student participating in the intervention two times a week for 20 minutes or five days a week for 30 minutes? The numbers make a difference. Look to the intervention to follow the described implementation suggestions. Follow-up training for teachers may be needed.

- **Is fluency really that important?**
    - Yes! We believe it is! We want students to be able to fluently decode without effort. This frees their thinking for comprehension. Reading to learn is what we want all students doing. As students progress in grade level, the text becomes more complex, there is more to read, and the words become more difficult to decode. We want students to read at a rate that is reasonable. If

something takes a long time to read, their stamina may diminish. Working on fluency now will help them later. We also have to make sure they are phrasing well. When they read assignments independently, we are assuming they are reading in phrases that allow for deep comprehension. Teachers need to check to see if this is the case.

- ◆ **I don't want my students to speed read and miss comprehension. Is this what happens when we test for oral reading fluency?**

  – We agree! Students should not be speed reading, and comprehension is absolutely the goal for all learners. The goal of increasing the fluency rate is not to read for speed, it is to read for automaticity. There is a big difference. We do not intend for students to read as fast as they can. We do intend for them to read with all of the components that encompass strong fluency. Using the oral reading probes to monitor progress is a way to ensure that fluency for students is increasing. It's up to us as educators to ensure this tool is being used correctly.

- ◆ **What if I give the phonics survey to students in Column 2, and they miss just a few items on the survey? Do they have to go to Column 3?**

  – The teacher will need to determine this. If there are just a couple of skills that seem to be missing, or if a child just needs a little more help in these areas, it may not be necessary for them to receive an intense phonics intervention. They may not need to be moved to Column 3. If the teacher decides to leave the student in Column 2 for a fluency intervention, the teacher should decide how the needed phonics skills will be delivered to the student. Other times of the day could be utilized. The teacher's judgment should be used in this case.

Note

* To review The Columns for Grades 2–5, see pages 11–12.

6

Column 3 for Grades 2–5*

The Importance of Phonics in the Reading Process

Phonics is a very important component of reading. The National Reading Panel report (2000) concluded that through examination of numerous studies that systematic and explicit phonics instruction makes a bigger contribution to children's growth in reading than alternative programs providing unsystematic or no phonics instruction. John Hattie (2009, p. 134) further reinforced through his meta-analysis of research the importance of phonics instruction, "Overall, phonics instruction is powerful in the process of learning to read – both for reading skills and reading comprehension." There are many books for educators that dive into all of the aspects related to phonics. For the purpose of our book, we want teachers to understand that phonics is a critical component, to identify phonics skills mastered and not mastered by students, and to understand that to remediate phonics skills, students should receive an intervention that has a strong scope and sequence taught in a systematic and explicit way. The National Reading Panel report (2000) states the following:

> For children with learning disabilities and children who are low achievers, systematic phonics instruction, combined with synthetic phonics instruction produced the greatest gains. Synthetic phonics instruction consists of teaching students to explicitly convert letters into phonemes and then blend the phonemes to form words.
>
> Moreover, systematic synthetic phonics instruction was significantly more effective in improving the reading skills of children from

low-socioeconomic levels. Across all grade levels, systematic synthetic phonics instruction improved the ability of good readers to spell.

(p. 5)

Column 3 for Grades 2–5

Column 3 for grades 2–5 helps teachers find students who have a foundational skill deficit in the reading component of phonics and perhaps phonological awareness. First, the teacher should give the universal screener determined by the school to all students. As mentioned previously, this might be AIMSweb, Acadience (formerly DIBELS), iReady, Fast Bridge, etc. Once the universal screener has been given, the teacher is first looking for students who fall in the 11th–24th percentiles. Scores in this range typically point to a deficient skill in the reading components of phonics and/or phonological awareness. Once a student is initially placed in Column 3 based on the universal screener percentile, the teacher must do two additional steps. One, an additional phonics survey is given to determine specific skill deficits in the scope and sequence of phonics, and two, the teacher must rule out or confirm deficits in the area of phonological awareness.

The first step for the teacher is to complete a phonics survey assessment. As mentioned in Chapter 5, there are several phonics survey assessments available. Some that we have seen used in schools include the 95 Percent Group PSI Phonics Screener for Intervention; the Quick Phonics Screener by Jan Hasbrouck; the Decoding Survey by Really Great Reading, along with a host of others. We do not promote one over the others; you can use the one that best fits your district. It is just important that you do have one available. Once you have identified the phonics survey tool you will use, this should be given to all students falling in Column 3. By giving this survey, the teacher is able to pinpoint exactly what phonics skills have been mastered by the student, and where the breakdown in skills occurs for the student. Once all students in this Column have been given the phonics screener, the teacher can group students by need in order to ensure the skill gap for phonics begins to be remediated.

One additional diagnostic that must be given by teachers for students falling in this Column is a phonological awareness diagnostic assessment. Teachers must ensure that the phonological awareness foundational component is in place for students. The only way to know that is to give this additional diagnostic. One such diagnostic is the PAST (Phonological Awareness Skills Test), or the 95 Percent Group's PASI (Phonological Awareness Screener for Intervention). There are others as well. Again, we don't promote one over the others. When choosing a phonological awareness diagnostic, be sure that the assessment checks for all components of phonological awareness. This diagnostic should check for understanding in concept of word; rhyming; syllables; onset/rime; isolation of initial, middle, and final sounds; blending; segmenting; addition; substitution; and deletion. By giving this additional assessment, the teacher is either ruling out a concern in this area (because the student passes the assessment), or confirming deficits in the area of phonological awareness (because the student does not master this assessment).

In Column 3, you will see an area for "phonics only" and an area for "phonics and phonological awareness." For students that pass the phonological awareness diagnostic assessment, you have confirmed that the students have mastered the foundational skills of phonological awareness, and thus will be placed in a "phonics only" group. For students showing deficits on the phonological awareness diagnostic assessment, you will add their names to the "phonics and phonological awareness" section. The teacher has now determined which students in Column 3 need both phonological and phonics intervention, and which students only need phonics intervention.

If a student is diagnosed as needing both components, phonics and phonological awareness, it is likely their scores on the phonics survey will be similar. Most of the time, if students have a need for both components, they do not perform well on the phonics survey. The same may not be true for students who do not pass the phonological awareness diagnostic. Students that do not pass the phonological awareness diagnostic may have various holes in their understanding. Generally, if students are falling in Column 3 and need both phonics and phonological awareness, their phonics mastery will be low. Of course, this is not the case for all students, but it will be likely for most.

Once the teacher has determined who just needs phonics and who needs both phonics and phonological awareness intervention, the teacher should group students with similar skills together so that the intervention materials can be matched to the needs of the learners. Direct, explicit instruction should be given to students so that the phonetic and/or phonological deficits can be mastered. We will examine this in action as we practice with data examples in Chapter 8.

> Columns Case #7
> Grades 2–5
> Column placement: Column 3
>
> Student: Olivia
> Grade: 4
> Data: Universal screener composite: 18th percentile
> Oral reading fluency: 28th percentile
> Phonics survey: Needs support for long vowels, vowel r
> Phonological awareness assessment: No needs found
> Most recent state testing: Basic (not to proficient)
> Common formative assessments: Scores around 60% on comprehension CFAs
>
> Instructional focus: The composite score falls within the range for Column 3. The fluency score is higher, falling within Column 2's range. However, after giving the phonics survey, support for phonics beginning with long vowels was shown to be a concern, which can slow fluency. Students in Column 3 will receive phonics instruction, so Olivia will be placed here. During a 30-minute intervention, long vowels will be addressed, including using connected text to support application of the skill. Upon further checking into comprehension, Olivia also lacks understanding of literal comprehension and retell of text. During Tier 1 small group instruction, fluency and retell will be a focus. In one literacy station outside of small group, Olivia will practice long vowel concepts.
>
> Materials: Olivia's teacher will use 95 Percent Group phonics intervention materials to support long vowel and r controlled vowel development. Olivia's teachers will access district materials for Tier 1 and literacy station activities.

Once the teacher has determined need in Column 3, s/he will need to determine the intervention that matches this need. We will share some interventions we have seen used in schools, but please remember that there are many to choose from. Sound Partners gives teachers ready-made lessons that match the area of phonics skills needed. Wilson Fundations is also a good resource for students needing explicit instruction in the component of phonics. The Florida Center for Reading Research website (www.fcrr.org) provides specific activities in the component of phonics. The 95 Percent Group also has phonics intervention materials. The teacher can access various grade levels to identify the skills needed, as measured by the phonics survey assessment. It might be necessary to use a grade level that is lower than the student's current grade level. Remember, this is to be expected. The phonics survey you have given identifies a gap in the understanding of the foundational skill of phonics. This means you may need to seek a lower grade level to find activities to remediate this skill. The activities on the FCRR website are excellent for any tutors that might volunteer in your room, or for parents that might request additional help at home.

For students needing both phonics and phonological awareness, the teacher will need to determine how to intervene for both components. Generally, phonological awareness activities are fairly quick to complete. A program we have seen used often is *Phonemic Awareness: The Skills That They Need to Help Them Succeed* by Michael Heggerty and Alisa VanHekken. These are quick, scripted lessons that can easily be done before a teacher begins a phonics intervention. Using the interventions you have available at your school for phonological awareness and phonics, determine how you will ensure the student receives instruction in both.

One additional thing to point out to teachers is that phonics should not be taught in isolation. The students need to practice phonics skills, but they must also be able to apply the skills in reading. Make sure you are finding time to read books controlled for the phonics skills the students are practicing. For example, if you are working on the /ou/ sound, find decodable books that help students apply these words in reading. Only working on skills in isolation will ensure the student difficulty in carrying the skill over into their reading. This is an important note to remember as you plan for intervention. Use the intervention to explicitly teach the deficient skill, but still guarantee the student has time to apply the skills taught when reading text.

Frequently Asked Questions about Column 3

- **What if all of my students in this Column have a need for phonological awareness intervention?**
    - This is possible, especially if you are just beginning this work. It is possible that these students have never been screened for phonological needs, so you may find several when you first begin this work. If you do, it will be important that these students receive intervention in both phonics and phonological awareness so that this gap begins to close.

- **What if students are just missing a few phonological skills? They have some areas mastered, but not others?**
    - This certainly happens. The teacher can choose to remediate in just that area of phonological awareness to close that gap, or the teacher can choose to put the child in a more robust intervention for phonological awareness. If it is just one or two areas, the teacher may choose the former. One other thing to consider is to

look at the child's writing. If writing skills are low, it is likely there are gaps in their understanding of phonological awareness.

- ◆ **Some of my students passed many levels of the phonics survey, and others knew very little. Can I group them all together in the same intervention?**

  – To remediate phonics skills, we recommend placing students in groups with similar needs. For example, if you have a group of students that all need short vowel work, place them together. If three of your students have mastered this skill, but need help with digraphs, place them together. There could be some overlap, depending on how your classroom data falls out. It could be that there is one student who doesn't quite fit in a group. We recommend placing them with students most similar. Allowing a child to do some review before moving on is better than skipping skills the student needs to master.

- ◆ **After I give the initial phonics survey and phonological awareness diagnostic, do I need to re-give those assessments each time I do a universal screener?**

  – No, it is not necessary to re-give the entire assessment. When schools initially begin this process, it will feel like there is a lot of assessment to complete. Students falling in Columns 2, 3, and 4 require additional assessments to be given in order to find the deficient skill. Once these have been completed, the teacher can monitor progress by starting where the student stopped mastering the skill. For example, if a student was given the phonics diagnostic at the beginning of the year, when it is time again to do the universal and The Columns suggest giving the phonics survey again, the teacher will pick up where the student left off during the last assessment window. For instance, if the child passed the short vowels, but did not pass the digraphs, you should start again with digraphs and continue forward. Remember that the goal is to find the deficient skill. Use the assessments to tell you what the child does and does not know, and then match the intervention that will remediate those skills.

- ◆ **Why do we need to do so many assessments for kids in Column 3?**

  – If you think of assessment as a medical model, it begins to make more sense. Think of the screener like a blood pressure test.

Every time you go to the doctor, your blood pressure is taken. When the reading is high, the doctor may want to look further into why this is by asking for additional tests to rule out or confirm something that may be causing the high reading. Essentially, we are doing the same thing with students. When we get a screener score that shows possible concern, we want to investigate further. We must know more in order to make the correct diagnosis. Just as a doctor would want to ensure the correct medication is prescribed for the identified medical problem, the teacher needs to ensure that the correct intervention is prescribed for the identified skill deficit. When this process is first used, more assessment is required. However, once the assessments are given, if scores are kept on students, less assessment is required as you move forward with the process. Finding a way to track and keep data will be important as you begin to collect information.

- **Should I teach with the intervention materials during my small group reading?**
    - This question can be tricky to answer. We don't recommend that any teachers choose not to teach the grade level standards. We believe the best case scenario is that the teacher focuses on grade level standards during small group reading, and uses the intervention materials during an intervention time in the day. We realize that not all schools have an additional 30 minutes for intervention per day. If this is your situation, you should balance teaching skills to remediate the deficit and the grade level standards. This means that some of your small group reading lessons will be skill-based. This is absolutely appropriate for students with these deficient skills. While we believe that our most struggling students should work with the most qualified teachers, we also recognize that some schools have excellent volunteers (sometimes even retired educators). If this is the case for you, allowing volunteers to help with these deficient skills is also a way to target skill remediation for students.

- **Could a student that falls in Column 3 pass the phonics survey?**
    - While not likely, we never say never. Each child is unique. It could be that a child has been given a lot of intervention in a skill-based phonics intervention and has the skills to decode, but is still

not reading fluently. In this case, their percentile on the universal screener may initially place them in Column 3. If this is the case, and you give the phonics screener and learn that a child does not have a phonics deficit, the child would be moved to Column 2 and would most likely need a fluency intervention.

- ♦ **Which is the best phonics and phonological intervention(s) to use?**
  - Teachers and districts often inquire about which is the best intervention to buy. There is not one magic key to unlocking a student's potential in reading. The power is in the systems of implementation that a district utilizes. One district could use an intervention program and be highly successful. The next district could use it and not see any student growth. Consider fidelity to program implementation, frequency of lessons, length of lessons, and whether the program is accurately matched to student data. A teacher may instruct an intervention program perfectly for the correct amount of time, but if the student's need is not addressed in that program, gains will not be made. Sites such as What Works Clearinghouse will provide some guidance in selection. We have listed numerous interventions so as not to promote any one, and knowing that the systems a school adopts will make all the difference for teachers and students.

- ♦ **How can I be sure I haven't missed any students that might need phonics intervention?**
  - Remember that in Column 2, we did the phonics survey to ensure there were no underlying phonics concerns for these students. If students are placed in Column 2 by using the universal screening percentile, and they actually have a phonics deficit, we will find them by giving the phonics survey. These students will be moved to Column 3 if they do not pass the phonics survey. If you have a reason to have concerns about students falling in Column 1, you can always choose to give a phonics survey to these students to ensure no one has been missed.

Note

* To review The Columns for Grades 2–5, see pages 11–12.

7

Column 4 for Grades 2–5*

Working with Our Most Struggling Learners

Educators know far too well that some students struggle with many elements of literacy. They can have multiple needs across the reading components of comprehension, fluency, phonics, and phonemic awareness. Teachers will often express a feeling of being overwhelmed at knowing where to start intervention or deciding which skill to address first. They may have tried various interventions but failed to make the amount of progress they desire. Many teachers bring data and a history of instructional attempts to the table, all with deep concern for the student and a wish to try anything to make it better.

    We have all been there. We know these students. Any educator will tell you the deep worry and concern that is felt for them. However, if we structure our data to drill down to specific need and match to the correct intervention, we will see gains for these students. These students are represented in Column 4.

    Column 4 denotes students that are below the 10th percentile on the universal screener. Overall composites fall at or below the 10th percentile. They are performing well below their peers. To find the root of the problem, we must look for specific skill deficits. Both phonics skills and the application of phonics skills to text will be low. In Chapter 6, phonics surveys were discussed. The phonics survey pinpoints where students fall in the scope and sequence of phonics skills. Beginning skills often include letter identification, letter sound, consonant-vowel-consonant, digraphs, and blends. These skills are taught in kindergarten and first grade, but there may be fourth and fifth grade students that still struggle. Some students may be farther up the phonics skill sequence and still be in this category. Educators should identify the specific skills a student needs to work on within this sequence in order to know where to begin within a phonics intervention.

The reading component of phonological awareness is generally also a deficit for students in this category. In Column 3, students may or may not have had an issue in this area. In Column 4, the concern is almost always present. Chapter 6 described using the phonological awareness diagnostic to pinpoint need within the scope and sequence of phonological awareness skills. An assessment such as this should be administered for any student in Column 4. By grades 4 and 5, students may have had enough intervention that they know some of the concepts, but most skills are still not secure. It is important to find out

---

Columns Case #8
Grades 2–5
Column placement: Column 4

Student: Brady
Grade: 5
Data: Universal screener composite: 8th percentile
Oral reading fluency: 6th percentile
Phonics survey: Need beginning with digraphs/blends
Phonological awareness diagnostic: Multiple concerns
Most recent state testing: Below basic
Common formative assessments: Scores around 20% on comprehension CFAs
District high frequency word assessment: Has 73 of the first 100 sight words
Note: Does not qualify for special education
Note: Is not an English learner

Instructional focus: Brady performs below the 10th percentile on universal screeners. There are great needs in phonics and phonological awareness. Brady's 45-minute, daily intervention period will reflect his need for digraphs and blends in phonics and will begin with initial sounds in phonemic awareness (assessment indicated as a first need in the sequence). Tier 1 small group instruction will utilize connected text related to digraphs and blends. The text should be high interest for fifth grade, but include these phonics pieces. A tutor provides an additional 15 minutes to work on an identified list of sight words. Comprehension will be instructed through Tier 1 whole group. Additional supports may be utilized at this time.

Materials: Brady's teacher will use Wilson materials to support the intervention time. Brady's teachers will access FCRR and district materials for all other activities.

which skills are known and which are not. When thinking of the missing pieces for these students, David Kilpatrick, 2016b, p. 18) elaborates, "Phoneme awareness is arguably the most common source of reading difficulties. The good news is that it is trainable." The focus of Column 4 intervention, therefore, includes phonological awareness alongside phonics activities.

The Steps for this Column Mirror Column 3

Once a student is initially placed in this Column, the teacher will follow the same process followed in Column 3. The teacher should give the phonics survey and the phonological awareness diagnostic to determine what skills are deficient for the child. You will see the same choices given in Column 3. There is a place to identify just phonics needs and a place to identify students with both phonics and phonological awareness needs. As children enter the fourth and fifth grades, the phonological needs may be less, but then again, they may not be. It is necessary to give both assessments to determine need.

How Do We Intervene for These Students?

We intervene in the same way we do with students in Column 3. Determine where the needs are and then choose the intervention that matches the deficit. For students at or below the 10th percentile, a more intense intervention may be needed. We have listed ideas such as the Wilson Reading System, Barton Reading, and Orton-Gillingham-based programs. The 95 Percent Group is another resource for intervention materials.

The intensity of the intervention should be considered prior to starting it and also as progress is being monitored. Intensity can be increased in a variety of ways. The first is by changing the group size. To increase the intensity, decrease the size of the group. Individual instruction would be more intense than a group of three to five, which in turn would be more intense than a larger group. Another way to increase intensity is to increase the duration of the intervention. Did the instruction last 20 minutes, 30 minutes, or 45 minutes? Students in Column 4 may need more time to master the concept. Intensity is further increased by the frequency of the intervention. Did the student participate three times per week or five times per week? Five times per week is recommended for students in Column 4. A final way to increase intensity is the number of skills instructed. Column 4 students may move more slowly through the skill sequence.

Frequently Asked Questions for Column 4

- **What makes Column 3 different from Column 4?**

  - These two Columns only differ by the initial screener with which students are placed in the Column. Column 3 identifies students who score between the 11th–24th percentiles. Column 4 identifies those that are falling at the 10th percentile or below. While kids in each Column likely have similar needs, kids in Column 4 are at a greater deficit and their skills are lower. We believe it is necessary to closely track those students falling this low so that they can be more easily monitored.

- **Are these students often special education students?**

  - You might find special education students falling here. You might also find students that have not been tested for special education falling here. It could be that these students have been in interventions for a long time, but perhaps they have not been in the right intervention and these skill deficits have never improved. Making a referral for special education is something that should be discussed in your district. It is important to follow the procedures and expectations of your district. Students falling in Column 4 should be very closely monitored regardless of whether or not they are in special education.

Note

* To review The Columns for Grades 2–5, see pages 11–12.

8

Case Studies for Each Grade Level

In this chapter, we will give one scenario for each grade level that will allow teacher teams to practice sorting students into Columns. For each grade level, you will see the same format. You will find a list of children in the class on the *data collection form*. On this form, for each child, you will see the percentile scored on the universal screener. There will also be information listed for additional diagnostics given, along with notes to think about for each child. This will help teachers think about why children are placed in each Column and what should be considered for each. The notes are meant to be helpful for readers to understand why decisions are made, and the notes contain extra ideas to consider as you analyze strengths and deficits for each child. Needed foundational reading skills are the same, regardless of grade level. If these foundational skills are deficient, regardless of the grade level of the student, they must be mastered. If they are not, the teacher should identify the deficit and match an intervention to remediate.

For each scenario, we mainly used the language from AIMSweb as we sorted for initial Column placement, though you will be able to substitute your screener into the forms so that you can adapt it for your school. For grades K-1, you will need to know what your school uses to measure letter names, letter sounds, and phonological awareness. You will need a percentile score for these subtests to know where to initially place students. Make sure your screener gives you this information. Starting in the second semester of first grade, we use oral reading fluency, or an overall composite score as the starting point for analysis. This remains the same for grades 2–5. Further, you will see where the phonics surveys and phonological awareness diagnostics fit into the analysis.

The next step on the *data collection form* is to sort students into Columns, using the notes on this document. You will see an example of children sorted into The Columns for each grade level. We encourage you to use a blank form to sort with teacher teams. The discussion will lead you to think through how to apply the data to The Columns. Once you have the students sorted, you can check your sorting against ours by reviewing The Columns answer sheet for each grade level.

In the final step, you will consider how to group students by need. For each grade level, you will see how children are sorted and special notes to consider as you plan groups. Further, you will see interventions listed by each group. Remember, we listed a few interventions that we have used in schools over the years. This is not meant to be a recommendation, but rather a place to start. You should take time to determine what interventions are available in your school, and best for your students, and then plug them into The Columns. If you find you are missing an intervention for a component, this is a good time to research what might work best for your students.

In summary, as you begin to work through case studies for each grade-level, you will need the following documents:

1. The Data Collection Form which includes the steps for grouping students.
2. The blank Columns for Practice Sorting.
3. The Answer Key for the Columns.

Lastly, there will always be a student that may not fit The Columns exactly. When this happens, we want to help! You can reach us at TheColumnsK5@gmail.com. Please don't hesitate to contact us. By hearing your feedback, we can help others problem-solve for all students.

Kindergarten Case Study

Data Collection Form for Kindergarten

Student	Universal Screening Percentile for Letter Naming	Universal Screening Percentile for Letter Sounds	Universal Screening Percentile for Phonological Awareness	Notes
Ben	6% (2)	0% (3)	0% (4)	Ben needs to work across all areas.
Ethan	10% (2)	5% (3)	0% (4)	Ethan is starting to learn letters, but has very few other early reading skills.
Julie	25% (2)	18% (3)	50% (1)	Julie is progressing with letters. She needs to work on letter sounds and how letters and sounds go together for alphabetic principle.
Isabella	40% (1)	25% (3)	40% (1)	Isabella has good skills. She should continue to work on letter sounds to continue to grow in this area.
Ashanti	95% (1)	95% (1)	99% (1)	Ashanti is most likely a reader. He shows no concerns in early reading skills.
Melinda	80% (1)	75% (1)	80% (1)	Melinda is most likely a reader. She is making good progress.
Mateo	80% (1)	15% (3)	10% (4)	Mateo knows his letters, but needs to concentrate on letter sounds and phonological skills.
Emilio	15% (2)	10% (3)	35% (4)	Emilio is beginning to develop her phonological skills, but needs work in all other areas.

(continued overleaf)

Continued

Student	Universal Screening Percentile for Letter Naming	Universal Screening Percentile for Letter Sounds	Universal Screening Percentile for Phonological Awareness	Notes
Olivia	58% (1)	45% (1)	80% (1)	Olivia has strong early phonological skills. She is coming along in letter names and sounds, but needs continued practice.
Lucas	78% (1)	10% (3)	15% (4)	Lucas knows letter names, but needs additional work in letter sounds and phonological awareness.
Chloe	99% (1)	99% (1)	99% (1)	Chloe is most likely a reader.
Randy	5% (2)	0% (3)	20% (4)	Randy lacks most basic early reading skills. He does have some phonological awareness, but needs additional practice.
Jaquan	50% (1)	42% (1)	70% (1)	Jaquan is doing well with phonological development. He is progressing in other areas.
Kiara	80% (1)	72% (1)	90% (1)	Kiara is progressing well in early reading skills.
Heather	65% (1)	40% (1)	80% (1)	Heather is strong in phonological skills. She can continue to work on letter sound practice.
Carla	99% (1)	99% (1)	99% (1)	Carla is most likely a reader.
Theresa	50% (1)	48% (1)	60% (1)	Theresa is progressing in all areas.

() denotes Columns placement

Step One

Using the blank kindergarten Columns on pages 66 and 67, match each percentile score to each Column above. You will see the Column the child fits into noted below each percentage. Note that a child can only be placed in Column 1 if they are at or above the 40th percentile in all other Columns.

Step Two

Create groups to determine how to place kids with needed skills together.
Continue with Tier 1 curriculum:
- Ashanti
- Melinda
- Olivia
- Chloe
- Kiara
- Carla

Also in Column 1, but not scoring as high as those above:
- Jaquan
- Heather
- Theresa

Enrichment: Continue to teach grade level standards; apply standards to books they are reading

Needs letters and sounds:
- Julie

Intervention ideas: Double Dose Fundations; Sound Partners Kindergarten; www.fcrr.org; and Orton-Gillingham

Needs letter sounds and phonological awareness:
- Mateo
- Lucas

Intervention ideas: Double dose of Fundations; Sound Partners Kindergarten; www.fcrr.org; Orton-Gillingham; Heggerty Phonological Curriculum

Needs letter sounds only:
- Isabella

Intervention ideas: www.fcrr.org

All needs (letter name, sounds, and phonological awareness):
- Ben
- Ethan
- Randy
- Emilio (*Emilio is close for phonological awareness)

Intervention ideas: Double dose of Fundations; Sound Partners Kindergarten; www.fcrr.org; Orton-Gillingham; Heggerty Phonological Curriculum

Step Three

We are ready to match the intervention to the group. You will see we have given examples. Again, these are simply samples of options. Use what interventions you have available in your school.

Kindergarten Columns for Practice Sorting

Column 1: Ready to read – phonics short vowels plus CVC	Column 2: Need letter naming	Column 3: Need letter sounds
Students in this column have mastered letters, letter sounds and phonemic awareness skills.	Students in this column cannot identify some or all letters.	Students in this column do not know some or all letter sounds.
Universal screener: ♦ Letter naming fluency at/above 40th percentile ♦ Letter sound fluency at/above 40th percentile ♦ Phoneme segmentation at/above 40th percentile ♦ Initial sound fluency at/above 40th percentile ♦ Composite score above 40th percentile	**Universal screener:** ♦ Letter naming fluency below 40th percentile	**Universal screener:** ♦ Letter sound fluency below 40th percentile
Possible enrichments (examples): ♦ Sound Partners ♦ Fundations	**Skill checklist:** ___Makes random errors ___Errors on upper-case letters ___Errors on lower-case letters ___Errors on letters going below the line ___Errors in letters in student's name ___Doesn't track correctly ___Return sweep ___Consistent error on a specific letter	**Skill checklist:** ___Makes random errors ___Errors on lower-case letters ___Errors on letters going below the line ___Errors in letters in student's name ___Doesn't track correctly ___Return sweep ___Consistent error on a specific letter
Your enrichment tools here:	**Possible interventions (examples):** ♦ Fundations (matched to student need) ♦ www.fcrr.org ♦ Sound Partners Kindergarten ♦ Orton-Gillingham	**Possible interventions (examples):** ♦ Fundations (matched to student need) ♦ www.fcrr.org ♦ Sound Partners Kindergarten ♦ Orton-Gillingham
Student names:	**Your intervention tools here:** **Student names:**	**Your intervention tools here:** **Student names:**

(continued overleaf)

Continued

Column 4: Need phonological awareness	Column 5: Need high frequency words	Teacher notes here:
Students in this column need help with phonemic awareness skills. **Universal screener:** ◆ Phoneme segmentation below 40th percentile ◆ Initial sound fluency below 40th percentile **Skill checklist:** ___Concept of word ___Rhyming words ___Syllables ___Onset/rime ___Isolation of initial sounds ___Isolation of middle sounds ___Isolation of final sounds ___Blending ___Segmenting ___Addition ___Substitution ___Deletion **Possible interventions (examples):** ◆ Heggerty ◆ www.fcrr.org ◆ LiPS **Your intervention tools here:** **Student names:**	Students in this column need support in identifying and application of basic sight words. **Student names:**	

Kindergarten Columns Answer Key

Column 1: Ready to read – phonics short vowels plus CVC
Students in this column have mastered letters, letter sounds and phonemic awareness skills.

Universal screener:
- Letter naming fluency at/above 40th percentile
- Letter sound fluency at/above 40th percentile
- Phoneme segmentation at/above 40th percentile
- Initial sound fluency at/above 40th percentile

Possible enrichments (examples):
- Sound Partners
- Fundations

Your enrichment tools here:

Student names:
Ashanti
Melinda
Olivia
Chloe
Kiara
Carla

Students closer to 40th percentile; watch more closely:

Jaquan
Heather
Theresa

Column 2: Need letter naming
Students in this column cannot identify some or all letters.

Universal screener:
- Letter naming fluency below 40th percentile

Skill checklist:
___Makes random errors
___Errors on upper-case letters
___Errors on lower-case letters
___Errors on letters going below the line
___Errors in letters in student's name
___Doesn't track correctly
___Return sweep
___Consistent error on a specific letter

Possible interventions (examples):
- Fundations (matched to student need)
- www.fcrr.org
- Sound Partners Kindergarten
- Orton-Gillingham

Your intervention tools here:

Student names:
Ben
Ethan
Julie
Emilio
Randy

Column 3: Need letter sounds
Students in this column do not know some or all letter sounds.

Universal screener:
- Letter sound fluency below 40th percentile

Skill checklist:
___Makes random errors
___Errors on lower-case letters
___Errors on letters going below the line
___Errors in letters in student's name
___Doesn't track correctly
___Return sweep
___Consistent error on a specific letter

Possible interventions (examples):
- Fundations (matched to student need)
- www.fcrr.org
- Sound Partners Kindergarten
- Orton-Gillingham

Your intervention tools here:

Student names:
Ben
Ethan
Julie
Isabella
Mateo
Emilio
Lucas
Randy

(continued overleaf)

Continued

Column 4: Need phonological awareness	Column 5: Need high frequency words	Teacher notes here:
Students in this column need help with phonemic awareness skills. **Universal screener:** ◆ Phoneme segmentation below 40th percentile ◆ Initial sound fluency below 40th percentile **Skill checklist:** ___Concept of word ___Rhyming words ___Syllables ___Onset/rime ___Isolation of initial sounds ___Isolation of middle sounds ___Isolation of final sounds ___Blending ___Segmenting ___Addition ___Substitution ___Deletion **Possible interventions (examples):** ◆ Heggerty ◆ www.fcrr.org ◆ LiPS **Your intervention tools here:** **Student names:** Ben Ethan Mateo Emilio Lucas Randy	Students in this column need support in identifying and application of basic sight words. **Student names:**	

First Grade Case Study

Data Collection Form for First Grade, First Semester

Student	Universal Screening Percentile for Phonological Awareness	Universal Screening Percentile Nonsense Words	Phonological Awareness Diagnostic *Areas of deficit	Notes
Myra	99% (1)	75% (1)		Myra is on track and is likely reading. Continue to give her application to text and work on comprehension strategies.
Jose	75% (1)	50% (1)		Jose is on track. Watch nonsense words. If his progress slows, do a phonics survey.
Demitri	50% (1)	50% (1)		Demitri is on track, but should be watched closely. He is just over the 40% cut-off.
Susan	75% (1)	20% (2)		Susan's phonological skills are strong. She needs work on letter/sound correspondence.
Phillip	5% (6)	10% (6)	Phillip is only able to count number of spoken words and rhyme.	Phillip needs help in foundational reading skills. Letter naming and letter sound assessments should be given to check these skills.
Natasha	25% (4)	35% (4)	Natasha has phonological needs in substitution and deletion.	Natasha needs additional support in both phonological awareness and letter/sound correspondence.

(continued overleaf)

Continued

Student	Universal Screening Percentile for Phonological Awareness	Universal Screening Percentile Nonsense Words	Phonological Awareness Diagnostic *Areas of deficit	Notes
Liam	15% (4)	25% (4)	Liam needs phoneme segmentation and ending sounds (stopped the test).	Liam needs phonological awareness and letter/sound correspondence. Checking letter names and letter sounds is recommended.
Rashad	80% (1)	90% (1)		Rashad has solid foundational skills and is likely a reader.
Devin	95% (1)	90% (1)		Devin has solid foundational skills and is likely a reader.
Maria	20% (3)	50% (3)	Maria has deficient skills in phoneme segmentation, deletion, and substitution.	Maria needs additional support in phonological awareness. She is progressing in letter/sound correspondence, but should be monitored.
Marissa	5% (6)	10% (6)	Marissa has deficient skills in concept of spoken word and rhyming (stopped the test).	Marissa needs a lot of support in phonological awareness and letter/sound correspondence. Letter naming and letter sounds should be checked.
Mitch	40% (1)	40% (1)		Mitch should be watched closely. His

(continued overleaf)

Continued

Student	Universal Screening Percentile for Phonological Awareness	Universal Screening Percentile Nonsense Words	Phonological Awareness Diagnostic *Areas of deficit	Notes
				percentiles place him in Column 1, but right at the cut-off, which should prompt the teacher to watch closely.
Mia	15% (5)	15% (5)	Mia has deficient skills in beginning sounds and phoneme segmentation (stopped the test).	Mia needs assistance in phonological awareness and letter/sound correspondence. Letter names and sounds should be checked.
Lillian	80% (1)	72% (1)		Lillian is progressing well in early reading skills.
Henry	65% (1)	40% (1)		Henry is strong in phonological skills. He should continue to work on letter/sound correspondence, as he scores just at the cut-off for Column 1.
Dylan	99% (1)	99% (1)		Dylan has solid early foundational reading skills and is most likely a reader.
Andrew	50% (1)	48% (1)		Andrew is progressing in all areas of early reading skills, but should be monitored.

Step One

Using the first grade Columns for the first semester on pages 77–79, match each percentile score to each Column. You will see the Column the child fits into noted below each percentage on the data collection form. Note that a child can only be in Column 1 if they are at or above the 40th percentile in all other columns.

Step Two

Create groups to determine how to place kids with needed skills together.

Column 1

Continue with Tier 1 curriculum; concentrate on applied phonics skills, comprehension and standards work (the information below denotes percentiles):
- Myra 99%; 75%
- Jose 75%; 50%
- Demitri 50%; 50%
- Rashad 80%; 90%
- Devin 95%; 90%
- Mitch 40%; 40%
- Lillian 80%; 72%
- Henry 65%; 40%
- Dylan 99%; 99%

Enrichment: Continue to teach grade level standards; apply standards to the books they are reading; ensure they are applying phonics skills as they decode

**Note: There is a wide range of abilities in the Column 1 group. There are kids that are reading very well, and those that are decoding well, but still need support. They all need continued comprehension work, but the teacher should group the students reading well and with little effort together so that they can read more complex text. Additional assessments for comprehension might be needed. Remember that sometimes a child this young can read the words very well but may or may not be comprehending at a high level.

Column 2

Needs beginning phonics and application to text:
- Susan
- Andrew

Intervention ideas: Double dose of Fundations; Sound Partners Kindergarten; www.fcrr.org; Orton-Gillingham

Column 3

Low in phonological awareness, higher in beginning phonics:
- Maria

**Note: This column sets apart those kids that are beginning to decode, but have low phonological awareness skills. These kids must be closely monitored because they can become memorizers. They can remember what a word is, but because their knowledge in sounds is lacking, they are unable to decode it or write it if they have not memorized it.

Intervention ideas: www.fcrr.org activities for phonological awareness; Heggerty Phonological Curriculum

Column 4

Low in phonological awareness, developing in beginning phonics:
- Natasha
- Liam

Intervention ideas: www.fcrr.org in phonological awareness and early phonics; Sound Partners; double dose of Fundations; Orton-Gillingham; Heggerty Phonological Curriculum

Column 5

Low in phonological awareness, phonics is 11–24%:
- Mia

Intervention ideas: Double dose of Fundations; Sound Partners Kindergarten; www.fcrr.org; Orton-Gillingham; Heggerty Phonological Curriculum

Column 6

Low in phonological awareness and beginning phonics:
- Phillip
- Marissa

Intervention ideas: Double dose of Fundations; Sound Partners Kindergarten; www.fcrr.org; Orton-Gillingham; Heggerty Phonological Curriculum

Step three

We are ready to match the intervention to the group. You will see we have given examples. Again, these are simply samples of options. Use what interventions you have available in your school.

Note for first grade, first semester Columns: First grade is a big year for beginning reading. These Columns have allowed the teacher to dissect the skills for each student in the room. Some kids are working on similar skills, but just have different levels of mastery. Columns 4 and 5 are very similar, but each Column represents a slightly different level of early phonics understanding. When deciding the phonics intervention, it will be important for the teacher to ensure the students are placed at the correct starting lesson in the program. Each phonics program will have a way to determine where to begin. All students in Columns 4, 5, and 6 are deficient in phonological awareness.

First Grade, First Semester for Practice Sorting

Column 1: Need to extend phonics work plus comprehension/standards work	**Column 2: Need beginning phonics and application to text**
Students in this column have phonological awareness and beginning phonics skills. These students can work on comprehension skills, extend farther into the phonics skills sequence beyond current grade level instruction, and make application to text with those new skills.	Students in this column have phonological awareness skills, but need to work on beginning phonics. Kids falling in this column will have different phonics needs. You will determine where the student falls within the scope and sequence of phonics. Once this is determined, you should group students according to these phonics skills.

For students in this column, complete the universal screener:
- Example: Phoneme segmentation fluency at/above 40th percentile
- Example: Nonsense word fluency at/above 40th percentile
- Example: Composite score at/above 40th percentile

Instructional focus: Application to text; identify comprehension skill; next phonics need in skills sequence

Possible enrichment (example)
- Application to text

Your enrichment tools here:

Student names:

For students in this column, complete the universal screener:
- Example: Phoneme segmentation fluency at/above 40th percentile
- Example: Nonsense word fluency below 40th percentile

Next steps:
- Complete the phonics survey to pinpoint where students are in the scope and sequence of phonics

Instructional focus: Phonics skill building; application of known phonics skills to text

Possible interventions (examples) (use guidelines of the intervention to find beginning instruction based on phonics survey):
- Fundations
- Sound Partners
- www.fcrr.org

Your intervention tools here:

Student names:

(continued overleaf)

Continued

Column 3: Need phonological awareness, has basic phonics	**Column 4: Need phonics and phonological awareness skills**
Students in this column master basic phonics skills. There is a deficit in phonological awareness skills.	Students in this column are low in both phonics and phonological awareness skills. **A distinction for this column is that students fall in the 25th through 39th percentiles in phonics.**
For students in this column, complete the universal screener: ◆ Example: Phoneme segmentation fluency below 40th percentile ◆ Example: Nonsense word fluency above 40th percentile	**For students in this column, complete the universal screener:** ◆ Example: Phoneme segmentation fluency below 40th percentile ◆ Example: Nonsense word fluency between 25th and 39th percentiles
Next steps: ◆ Complete the phonological awareness diagnostic to pinpoint where students are in the scope and sequence of phonological awareness	**Next steps:** ◆ Complete the phonics survey to pinpoint where students are in the scope and sequence of phonics ◆ Complete the phonological awareness diagnostic to pinpoint where students are in the scope and sequence of phonological awareness
Instructional focus: Specific skills in the phonological awareness scope and sequence	**Instructional focus:** Phonics skill building; application of known phonics skills to text
Possible interventions (examples) (use guidelines of the intervention to find beginning instruction based on PA diagnostic): ◆ Phonological awareness: Heggerty, fcrr.org, LiPS	**Possible interventions (examples) (use guidelines of the intervention to find beginning instruction based on phonics survey and PA diagnostic):** ◆ Phonological awareness: Heggerty, fcrr.org, LiPS ◆ Phonics: Fundations, Sound Partners, Wilson Reading System, Barton Reading, Orton-Gillingham
Your intervention tools here:	**Your intervention tools here:**
Student names:	**Student names:**

(continued overleaf)

Continued

Column 5: Need basic phonics and phonological awareness Students in this column are low in both phonics and phonological awareness skills. Students know letters and letter sounds. **A distinction is that students in this column fall in between the 11th and 24th percentiles.** **For students in this column, complete the universal screener:** ◆ Example: Phoneme segmentation fluency below 40th percentile ◆ Example: Nonsense word fluency between 11th and 24th percentiles **Next steps:** ◆ Complete the phonics survey to pinpoint where students are in the scope and sequence of phonics ◆ Complete the phonological awareness diagnostic to pinpoint where students are in the scope and sequence of phonological awareness **Instructional focus:** Specific skills in phonics and phonological awareness scope and sequence **Possible interventions (examples) (use guidelines of the intervention to find beginning instruction based on phonics survey and PA diagnostic):** ◆ Phonics: Fundations; Sound Partners; Orton-Gillingham ◆ Phonological awareness: Heggerty; fcrr.org; LiPS **Your intervention tools here:** **Student names:**	**Column 6: May need work with letter identification and letter sounds plus very beginning phonics plus phonological awareness** Students in this column may need support with identifying some letters and/or letter sounds. They need support with phonological awareness and the very beginning skills in the phonics sequence. **A distinction is that students in this column fall below the 10th percentile in phonics.** **For students in this column, complete the universal screener:** ◆ Example: Phoneme segmentation fluency below 40th percentile ◆ Example: AIMSweb nonsense word fluency below 10th percentile **Next steps:** ◆ Complete the phonics survey to pinpoint where students are in the scope and sequence of phonics ◆ Complete the phonological awareness diagnostic to pinpoint where students are in the scope and sequence of phonological awareness ◆ If letter naming fluency and letter sound fluency are not included in the phonics survey or phonological awareness diagnostic, then administer separately **Instructional focus:** Letter identification and letter sound; specific skills in phonological awareness scope and sequence **Possible interventions (examples):** ◆ Phonics: Fundations; LiPS; letter recognition and letter/sound correspondence; Wilson Reading System; Barton Reading; Orton-Gillingham ◆ Phonological awareness: Heggerty **Your intervention tools here:** **Student names:**

First Grade, First Semester
First Grade, First Semester Answer Key

Column 1: Need to extend phonics work plus comprehension/standards work	**Column 2: Need beginning phonics and application to text**
Students in this column have phonemic awareness and beginning phonics skills. These students can work on comprehension skills, extend farther into the phonics skills sequence beyond current grade level instruction, and make application to text with those new skills.	Students in this column have phonemic awareness skills, but need to work on beginning phonics. Kids falling in this column will have different phonics needs. You will determine where the student falls within the scope and sequence of phonics. Once this is determined, you should group students according to these phonics skills.

Column 1 (continued):

For students in this column, complete the universal screener:
- Example: AIMSweb phoneme segmentation fluency at/above 40th percentile
- Example: AIMSweb nonsense word fluency at/above 40th percentile
- Example: Composite score 40th at/above percentile

Instructional focus: Application to text; identify comprehension skill, next phonics need in skills sequence

Possible enrichment (example):
- Application to text

Your enrichment tools here:

Student names:
- Myra 99%; 75%
- Rashad 80%; 90%
- Devin 95%; 90%
- Lillian 80%; 72%
- Dylan 99%; 99%

Students closer to 40th percentile; watch more closely:
- Jose 75%; 50%
- Demitri 50%; 50%
- Mitch 40%; 40%
- Henry 65%; 40%

Column 2 (continued):

For students in this column, complete the universal screener:
- Example: AIMSweb phoneme segmentation fluency at/above 40th percentile
- Example: AIMSweb nonsense word fluency below 40th percentile

Next steps:
- Complete the phonics survey to pinpoint where students are in the scope and sequence of phonics

Instructional focus: Phonics skill building; application of known phonics skills to text

Possible interventions (examples) (use guidelines of the intervention to find beginning instruction based on phonics survey):
- Fundations
- Sound Partners
- www.fcrr.org

Your intervention tools here:

Student names:
- Susan
- Andrew

(continued overleaf)

Continued

Column 3: Need phonemic awareness, has basic phonics	Column 4: Need phonics and phonemic awareness skills
Students in this column master basic phonics skills. There is a deficit in phonological/phonemic awareness skills. **For students in this column, complete the universal screener:** ◆ Example: AIMSweb phoneme segmentation fluency below 40th percentile ◆ Example: AIMSweb nonsense word fluency above 40th percentile **Next steps:** ◆ Complete the phonological awareness diagnostic to pinpoint where students are in the scope and sequence of phonological awareness **Instructional focus:** Specific skills in the phonological awareness scope and sequence. **Possible intervention (example) (use guidelines of the intervention to find beginning instruction based on PA diagnostic):** ◆ Phonemic awareness: Heggerty; fcrr.org **Your intervention tools here:** **Student names:** ◆ Maria	Students in this column are low in both phonics and phonemic awareness skills. **A distinction for this column is that students fall in the 25th through 39th percentiles in phonics.** **For students in this column, complete the universal screener:** ◆ Example: AIMSweb phoneme segmentation fluency below 40th percentile ◆ Example: AIMSweb nonsense word fluency between 25th and 39th percentiles **Next steps:** ◆ Complete the phonics survey to pinpoint where students are in the scope and sequence of phonics ◆ Complete the phonological awareness diagnostic to pinpoint where students are in the scope and sequence of phonological awareness **Instructional focus:** Phonics skill building; application of known phonics skills to text **Possible interventions (examples) (use guidelines of the intervention to find beginning instruction based on phonics survey and PA diagnostic):** ◆ Phonics: Fundations; Sound Partners; www.fcrr.org ◆ Phonemic awareness: Heggerty; fcrr.org **Your intervention tools here:** **Student names:** ◆ Natasha ◆ Liam

(continued overleaf)

Continued

Column 5: Need basic phonics and phonemic awareness	Column 6: May need work with letter identification and letter sounds plus very beginning phonics plus phonemic awareness
Students in this column are low in both phonics and phonemic awareness skills. Students know letters and letter sounds. **A distinction is that students in this column fall in between the 11th and 24th percentiles.** **For students in this column, complete the universal screener:** ◆ Example: AIMSweb phoneme segmentation fluency below 40th percentile ◆ Example: AIMSweb nonsense word fluency between 11th and 24th percentiles **Next steps:** ◆ Complete the phonics survey to pinpoint where students are in the scope and sequence of phonics ◆ Complete the phonological awareness diagnostic to pinpoint where students are in the scope and sequence of phonological awareness **Instructional focus:** Specific skills in phonics and phonological awareness scope and sequence **Possible interventions (examples) (use guidelines of the intervention to find beginning instruction based on phonics survey and PA diagnostic):** ◆ Phonics: Fundations; Sound Partners; Orton-Gillingham ◆ Phonemic awareness: Heggerty; fcrr.org; LiPS **Your intervention tools here:** **Student names:** ◆ Mia	Students in this column may need support with identifying some letters and/or letter sounds. They need support with phonemic awareness and the very beginning skills in the phonics sequence. **A distinction is that students in this column fall below the 10th percentile in phonics.** **For students in this column, complete the universal screener:** ◆ Example: AIMSweb phoneme segmentation fluency below 40th percentile ◆ Example: AIMSweb nonsense word fluency below 10th percentile **Next steps:** ◆ Complete the phonics survey to pinpoint where students are in the scope and sequence of phonics ◆ Complete the phonological awareness diagnostic to pinpoint where students are in the scope and sequence of phonological awareness ◆ If letter naming fluency and letter sound fluency are not included in the phonics survey or phonological awareness diagnostic, then administer separately **Instructional focus:** Letter identification and letter sound; specific skills in phonological awareness scope and sequence **Possible interventions (examples):** ◆ Phonics: Fundations; LiPS; letter recognition and letter/sound correspondence; Wilson Reading System; Barton Reading; Orton-Gillingham ◆ Phonological awareness: Heggerty **Your intervention tools here:** **Student names:** ◆ Phillip ◆ Marissa

Data Collection Form for First Grade, Second Semester

Student	Universal Screening Percentile for Oral Reading or Composite	Phonological Awareness Diagnostic *Areas of Deficit	Phonics Survey *Areas of Deficit	Notes
Gabby	75% (1)			Gabby is a reader. Continue to give her application to text and work on comprehension strategies.
Asher	5% (4)	Asher is unable to complete any parts of the phonological awareness diagnostic.	Asher knows some letters and no sounds.	Asher has very deficient foundational reading skills. Continue to work on phonological awareness, letters and letter sounds.
Amanda	45% (1)			Amanda is moving along. Continue to assist with beginning phonics and make sure she is applying these skills to text. Continue with comprehension and grade level standards.
Cody	34% (2)	Given – student passed the test.	Cody knows letter names and sounds. Deficits in short vowels and digraphs.	Cody needs additional intervention in beginning phonics to improve his skills.
Violet	75% (1)			Violet is a reader. Continue to give her application to text and work on

(continued overleaf)

Continued

Student	Universal Screening Percentile for Oral Reading or Composite	Phonological Awareness Diagnostic *Areas of Deficit	Phonics Survey *Areas of Deficit	Notes
				comprehension strategies.
Xavier	24% (3)	Given – student passed the test.	Xavier knows letter names and sounds, but needs short vowels and digraphs.	Xavier needs additional intervention in beginning phonics to improve his skills.
Alice	12% (3)	Alice has deficient skills in ending sounds, substitution, and deletion.	Alice knows letters and sounds, but needs additional work on short vowels.	Alice needs phonological awareness and letter/sound correspondence. She needs additional practice reading CVC words, and then applying that to controlled, decodable text.
Sadie	23% (3)	Given – student passed the test.	Sadie knows letters and sounds, but needs additional work on short vowels.	Sadie has phonological awareness skills, but needs additional practice with reading CVC words, and then applying that to controlled, decodable text.
Lucia	99% (1)			Lucia is a reader. Continue to expand his reading choices and ensure he is

(continued overleaf)

Continued

Student	Universal Screening Percentile for Oral Reading or Composite	Phonological Awareness Diagnostic *Areas of Deficit	Phonics Survey *Areas of Deficit	Notes
				comprehending at grade level.
Leo	50% (1)			Leo is moving along. Continue to assist with beginning phonics and make sure he is applying these skills to text. Continue with comprehension and grade level standards.
Daniela	0% (4)	Daniela has deficient skills in rhyming and beginning sounds (stopped the test).	Daniela does not know all of her letters or letter sounds.	Daniela needs a lot of support in phonological awareness and letter names and sounds.
Paula	9% (4)	Paula has deficient skills in phoneme segmentation (stopped the test).	Paula knows her letters but not all letter sounds.	Paula needs additional support in phonological awareness and letter sounds.
Malik	28% (2)	Given – student passed the test.	Malik knows letters, letter sounds, and short vowels. Needs digraphs.	Malik has phonological awareness skills. He needs additional work on decoding words with digraphs. Use connected, decodable text.
Hunter	86% (1)			Hunter is a reader. Continue to expand

(continued overleaf)

Continued

Student	Universal Screening Percentile for Oral Reading or Composite	Phonological Awareness Diagnostic *Areas of Deficit	Phonics Survey *Areas of Deficit	Notes
				his reading choices and ensure he is comprehending at grade level.
Jamal	30% (2)	Given – student passed the test.	Jamal knows letters and sounds, but needs help with digraphs.	Jamal has phonological awareness skills. He needs additional work on decoding words with digraphs. Use connected, decodable text.
Kiara	41% (1)			Kiara's universal screening score places her in Column 1. The teacher should watch her closely to ensure she continues to progress. If progression stalls, the teacher should consider the phonics survey to look for possible missing skills.
Diamond	64% (1)			Diamond is progressing well. Continue to expand her reading choices and ensure she is comprehending at grade level.

Step One
Using the first grade Columns for the second semester, match each percentile score to each Column. You will see the Column the child fits into noted below each percentage on the data collection form.

Step Two
Create groups to determine how to place kids with needed skills together.

Column 1
Continue with Tier 1 curriculum; concentrate on applied phonics skills, comprehension and standards work:
- Gabby 75%
- Violet 75%
- Lucia 99%
- Hunter 86%
- Diamond 64%
- Amanda 45%
- Leo 50%
- Kiara 41%

Enrichment: Continue to teach grade level standards; apply standards to books they are reading; ensure they are applying phonics skills as they decode

**Note: There is a wide range of abilities in the Column 1 group. There are kids that are reading very well, and others that are decoding well, but still need support. They all need continued comprehension work, but the teacher should group the students reading well and with little effort together so that they can read more complex text. Additional assessments for comprehension might be needed. Remember that sometimes a child this young can read the words very well but may or may not be comprehending at a high level.

Column 2
Needs beginning phonics and application to text:
- Cody
- Malik
- Jamal

Intervention ideas: Double dose of Fundations; www.fcrr.org (specific to phonics skills needed); Orton-Gillingham; fluency practice

Column 3
Needs basic phonics and possibly phonological awareness:
- **Phonics only:**
  - Xavier
  - Sadie
- **Phonics and phonological awareness:**
  - Alice

Intervention ideas: Double dose of Fundations; www.fcrr.org (specific to phonics/phonological skills needed); Orton-Gillingham; Heggerty Phonological Curriculum

Column 4
Needs letter names and sounds:
- Asher
- Daniela
- Paula

Intervention ideas: Double dose of Fundations; www.fcrr.org (specific to phonics/phonological awareness skills needed); Orton-Gillingham; Heggerty Phonological Curriculum

Step Three
We are ready to match the intervention to the group. You will see we have given examples. Again, these are simply samples of options. Use what interventions you have available in your school.

Note for first grade, second semester Columns: First grade is a big year for beginning reading. First semester Columns allowed the teacher to dissect the skills for each student in the room. If you have information from the first semester and have collected data on phonological awareness, you can use that to determine if a child is secure in phonological development. Meaning, you may not need to give the phonological diagnostic to every child if you have been watching this skill throughout the first semester. The one element this assessment would add to a teacher's knowledge base is to know what skills within phonological awareness are deficient. When deciding where to start kids in a phonics program, remember to follow the program guidelines so that you are sure they are beginning with the skills they need.

First Grade, Second Semester for Practice Sorting

Column 1: Need to extend phonics work plus comprehension/standards work	Column 2: Need beginning phonics and application to text
Students in this column have phonemic awareness and beginning phonics skills. These children are able to read connected text at an appropriate rate according to grade level assessment. They are fluent. These students can work on comprehension skills, extend farther into the phonics skills sequence beyond current grade level instruction, and make application to text with those new skills.	Students in this column have phonemic awareness skills. They mastered some basic phonics skills, but are low in rate of fluency. They need to fluently read the phonics skills that they have mastered. Determine where the student falls within the scope and sequence of phonics. Once this is determined, you should group students according to these phonics skills and work to increase fluent application of phonics and decoding skills to text.
For students in this column, complete the universal screener: ◆ Example: AIMSweb oral reading at/above 40th percentile ◆ Example: Composite score at/above 40th percentile	**For students in this column, complete the universal screener:** ◆ Example: AIMSweb oral reading between 25th and 39th percentiles ◆ Example: Composite score between 25th and 39th percentiles
Instructional focus: Application to text; identify comprehension skill; next phonics need in skills sequence	**Next steps:** ◆ Complete the phonics survey – no phonics concerns should be found for Column 2 ◆ Complete the phonological awareness diagnostic – no concerns should be found for Column 2
Possible enrichment (example): ◆ Application to text	**Instructional focus:** Application of known phonics skills to text; increase in rate of fluency
Your intervention tools here:	**Possible intervention resources/materials (examples):** ◆ Fundations ◆ www.fcrr.org
Student names:	**Your intervention tools here:**
	Student names:

(continued overleaf)

Continued

Column 3: Need basic phonics and possibly phonological awareness skills	Column 4: Need work with letter identification and letter sounds
Students in this column are low in both phonics and phonemic awareness skills. Students have not mastered some basic phonics skills. Students know letters and letter sounds. **For students in this column, complete the universal screener:** ♦ Example: AIMSweb oral reading between 11th and 24th percentiles ♦ Example: Composite between 11th and 24th percentiles **Next steps:** ♦ Complete the phonics survey to pinpoint where students are in the scope and sequence of phonics ♦ Complete the phonological awareness diagnostic to pinpoint where students are in the scope and sequence of phonological awareness **Instructional focus:** Specific skills in phonics and phonological awareness scope and sequence **Possible interventions (examples):** ♦ Phonics: Sound Partners; Fundations; Orton-Gillingham ♦ Phonological awareness: Heggerty; www.fcrr.org (match need to areas of deficit on the phonological awareness survey); LiPS **Your intervention tools here:** **Student names – phonics only:** **Student names – phonics and phonological awareness:**	Students in this column need support with identifying some letters and/or letter sounds. They also need support with phonological awareness. **For students in this column, complete the universal screener:** ♦ Example: AIMSweb oral reading below 10th percentile ♦ Example: Composite below 10th percentile **Next steps:** ♦ Complete the phonics survey to pinpoint where students are in the scope and sequence of phonics ♦ Complete the phonological awareness diagnostic to pinpoint where students are in the scope and sequence of phonological awareness **Instructional focus:** Specific skills in the phonological awareness scope and sequence; fluency of letter identification and letter sound **Possible interventions (examples):** ♦ Phonics: Sound Partners; Fundations; letter recognition and letter/sound correspondence; Wilson Reading System; Barton Reading; Orton-Gillingham ♦ Phonological awareness: Heggerty; LiPS **Your intervention tools here:** **Student names:**

First Grade, Second Semester
First Grade, Second Semester Answer Key

Column 1: Need to extend phonics work plus comprehension/standards work	**Column 2: Need beginning phonics and application to text**
Students in this column have phonemic awareness and beginning phonics skills. These children are able to read connected text at an appropriate rate according to grade level assessment. They are fluent. These students can work on comprehension skills, extend farther into the phonics skills sequence beyond current grade level instruction, and make application to text with those new skills.	Students in this column have phonemic awareness skills. They mastered some basic phonics skills, but are low in rate of fluency. They need to fluently read the phonics skills that they have mastered. Determine where the student falls within the scope and sequence of phonics. Once this is determined, you should group students according to these phonics skills and work to increase fluent application of phonics and decoding skills to text.
For students in this column, complete the universal screener: ◆ Example: AIMSweb oral reading at/above 40th percentile ◆ Example: Composite score at/above 40th percentile	**For students in this column, complete the universal screener:** ◆ Example: AIMSweb oral reading between 25th and 39th percentiles ◆ Example: Composite score between 25th and 39th percentiles
Enrichment focus: Application to text; identify comprehension skill; next phonics need in skills sequence	**Next steps:** ◆ Complete the phonics survey – no phonics concerns should be found for Column 2 ◆ Complete the phonological awareness diagnostic – no concerns should be found for Column 2
Possible interventions (examples): ◆ Application to text ◆ Fundations	**Instructional focus:** Application of known phonics skills to text; increase in rate of fluency
Your intervention tools here:	**Possible intervention resources/materials (examples):** ◆ Fundations ◆ www.fcrr.org
Student names: ◆ Gabby 75% ◆ Violet 75% ◆ Lucia 99% ◆ Hunter 86% ◆ Diamond 64%	**Your intervention tools here:**
Students close to the 40th percentile; watch more closely: ◆ Amanda 45% ◆ Leo 50% ◆ Kiara 41%	**Student names:** ◆ Cody ◆ Malik ◆ Jamal

(continued overleaf)

Continued

Column 3: Need basic phonics and phonemic awareness skills	**Column 4: Need work with letter identification and letter sounds**
Students in this column are low in both phonics and phonemic awareness skills. Students have not mastered some basic phonics skills. Students know letters and letter sounds.	Students in this column need support with identifying some letters and/or letter sounds. They also need support with phonological awareness.
For students in this column, complete the universal screener: ◆ Example: AIMSweb oral reading between 11th and 24th percentiles ◆ Example: Composite between the 11th and 24th percentiles	**For students in this column, complete the universal screener:** ◆ Example: AIMSweb oral reading below 10th percentile ◆ Example: Composite below 10th percentile
Next steps: ◆ Complete the phonics survey to pinpoint where students are in the scope and sequence of phonics ◆ Complete the phonological awareness diagnostic to pinpoint where students are in the scope and sequence of phonological awareness	**Next steps:** ◆ Complete the phonics survey to pinpoint where students are in the scope and sequence of phonics ◆ Complete the phonological awareness diagnostic to pinpoint where students are in the scope and sequence of phonological awareness
Instructional focus: Specific skills in phonics and phonological awareness scope and sequence	**Instructional focus:** Specific skills in the phonological awareness scope and sequence; fluency of letter identification and letter sound
Possible interventions (examples): ◆ Phonics: Sound Partners; Fundations; Orton-Gillingham ◆ Phonological awareness: Heggerty; www.fcrr.org (match need to areas of deficit on the phonological awareness survey); LiPS	**Possible interventions (examples):** ◆ Phonics: Sound Partners; Fundations; letter recognition and letter/sound correspondence; Wilson Reading System; Barton Reading; Orton-Gillingham ◆ Phonological awareness: Heggerty; LiPS
Your intervention tools here:	**Your intervention tools here:**
Student names – phonics only: ◆ Xavier ◆ Sadie **Student names – phonics and phonemic awareness:** ◆ Alice	**Student names:** ◆ Asher ◆ Daniela ◆ Paula

Second Grade Case Study

Data Collection Form for Second Grade

Student	Universal Screening Percentile for Oral Reading or Composite Score	Basic Comprehension or Standards Work (Column 1)	Phonological Awareness Diagnostic *Areas of deficit	Phonics Survey *Areas of deficit	Notes
William	84% (1)	Standards work			William is scoring high on the universal screener. He should continue to work on grade level standards.
Ava	34% (2)			Given – student passed the test.	Ava passed the phonics survey which means she does not have a phonics deficit. She should remain in Column 2 and receive a fluency intervention.
Mason	27% (2) *Move to Column 3, based on phonics survey information.		Given – student passed the test.	Mason did not pass vowel teams.	Mason should be moved to Column 3 due to his results on the phonics screener. This result also triggered a check for phonological skills. He did pass this diagnostic, so only needs additional phonics work. Place him in "phonics only."
Charlotte	8% (4)		Charlotte did not pass phoneme segmentation, ending	Charlotte passed letter name and sounds,	Charlotte has deficient skills in phonological awareness and phonics. She

(continued overleaf)

Continued

Student	Universal Screening Percentile for Oral Reading or Composite Score	Basic Comprehension or Standards Work (Column 1)	Phonological Awareness Diagnostic *Areas of deficit	Phonics Survey *Areas of deficit	Notes
			sounds, substitution, or deletion.	but did not pass short vowels.	should be placed in this section of Column 4 and receive intervention for both components.
Ebony	42% (1)	Basic comprehension			Ebony is in Column 1, but still struggles with basic comprehension. She is reading at a reasonable rate, but needs to work on comprehension.
James	52% (1)	Standards work			We should watch James closely. He falls close to the 40% cut-off. He seems to do okay on basic comprehension, so continue with standards work, but keep a close eye on him.
Aliyah	75% (1)	Standards work			Aliyah is doing well and should continue to deeply develop grade level standards.
DeShawn	99% (1)	Standards work			DeShawn is a high-performing student. Continue to give

(continued overleaf)

Continued

Student	Universal Screening Percentile for Oral Reading or Composite Score	Basic Comprehension or Standards Work (Column 1)	Phonological Awareness Diagnostic *Areas of deficit	Phonics Survey *Areas of deficit	Notes
					him more complex text around standards at and above grade level.
Ethan	15% (3)		Ethan has deficient skills in ending sounds, deletion, and substitution.	Ethan passed letter naming and sounds. He has deficits in short vowels, digraphs, and blends.	Ethan is just above the cut-off for Column 4. He is a student we should watch very closely. He should be in interventions for both phonological awareness and phonics.
Deja	23% (3)		Deja passed the phonological diagnostic.	Deja passed letter names, sound, and short vowels. She did not pass blends and digraphs.	Deja should be placed in Column 3, phonics only. Match her with other students who need blend and digraph work.
Nia	16% (3)		Nia has deficient skills in syllables, ending sounds, substitution, and deletion.	Nia passed letter names and sounds, but does not have short vowels mastered.	Nia should be placed in Column 3, phonics and phonological awareness. She needs intervention in both components.

(continued overleaf)

Continued

Student	Universal Screening Percentile for Oral Reading or Composite Score	Basic Comprehension or Standards Work (Column 1)	Phonological Awareness Diagnostic *Areas of deficit	Phonics Survey *Areas of deficit	Notes
Brett	40% (1)	Basic comprehension			Brett just barely made the cut-off for Column 1. He needs additional work on basic comprehension strategies.
Cole	88% (1)	Standards work			Cole is progressing well and should continue to work on complex text with grade level standards at and above grade level.
Stella	38% (2)			Stella passed the phonics survey.	Stella is placed correctly and should remain in Column 2 for additional fluency intervention.
Leah	9% (4)		Leah has deficient skills in rhyming, and beginning sounds (stopped the test because of difficulty).	Leah knows her letters, she does not know letter sounds.	Leah is in Column 4 and needs basic letter sound work and phonological awareness intervention.
Brooklyn	9% (4)		Brooklyn passed the phonological diagnostic.	Brooklyn does not know letter names or sounds.	Brooklyn passed the phonological diagnostic, but needs letter names and sounds. She should be placed in Column 4, phonics only.

(continued overleaf)

Continued

Student	Universal Screening Percentile for Oral Reading or Composite Score	Basic Comprehension or Standards Work (Column 1)	Phonological Awareness Diagnostic *Areas of deficit	Phonics Survey *Areas of deficit	Notes
Elijah	5% (4)		Elijah has deficient skills in beginning sounds and ending sounds (stopped the test because of difficulty).	Elijah does not know letter names or sounds.	Elijah is in Column 4 and needs letter names, letter sounds, and phonological awareness interventions.

Step One

Using the second through fifth grade Columns, match each percentile score to the percentile range on the Columns. If the child has been given additional assessments, you will see that listed. This information may change Column placement.

Step Two

Create groups to determine how to place kids with needed skills together.

Column 1

Standards work:
- William 84%
- James 52%
- Aliyah 75%
- DeShawn 99%
- Cole 81%

Basic comprehension and standards work:
- Ebony 42%
- Brett 40%

**Note: James is an outlier in Column 1 standards work, only because his universal screener was 52%. He does not present as having basic comprehension problems, and he may need extra support compared to others in his group. The teacher will need to determine how these seven kids best fit together according to their needs. Additional assessments such as common assessments or comprehension assessments may be needed to determine this.

Enrichment: Continue to teach complex text using grade level standards; apply standards to books they are reading

Column 2
Needs fluency:
- Ava
- Stella

Intervention ideas: Read Naturally; Fluency Formula

Column 3
Needs phonics:
- Mason
- Deja

Needs phonological awareness and phonics:
- Ethan
- Nia

Intervention ideas: Double dose of Fundations; Sound Partners Kindergarten; www.fcrr.org; Orton-Gillingham; Heggerty Phonological Curriculum

Column 4
Below 10% in phonics and/or phonological

Needs phonics:
- Brooklyn

Needs phonological awareness and phonics:
- Charlotte
- Leah
- Elijah

Intervention ideas: Double dose of Fundations; Wilson Reading System; Barton Reading; Orton-Gillingham; Heggerty Phonological Curriculum

**Note: It may be possible to combine students in Columns 3 and 4 when creating intervention groups. Using the interventions you have available in your school, determine where each child should start in the lesson progression of the intervention. If students in these Columns fall together, it is fine to place them together. The reason we created a distinction for Columns 3 and 4 is because the teacher should pay very close attention to those students below the 10th percentile. By giving them their own column, it allows the teacher to track them closely.

Step Three

We are ready to match the intervention to the group. You will see we have given examples. Again, these are simply samples of options. Use what interventions you have available in your school. The teacher should list the interventions available and create groups, then decide who will teach this group.

Second Through Fifth Grade Columns for Practice Sorting

Column 1: Comprehension/standards work needed – students are fluent and accurate Students in this column have phonics, are fluent readers, but need to continue to work on grade level standards **For students in this column, complete the universal screener:** ♦ Example: Oral reading fluency at/above 40th percentile ♦ Example: Composite score at/above 40th percentile **To identify the instructional focus:** ♦ Common formative assessments aligned to state standards ♦ Vocabulary if your screener assesses this component **Possible enrichments (top of the Column)/ interventions (bottom of the Column):** ♦ Standards work-identified prioritized standards ♦ Vocabulary ♦ Student's next steps may be enrichment related to the standards OR it could be intervention on basic comprehension plus standards work (PALS, Making Meaning, Strategies that Work Toolkit) ♦ Standards-based websites **Student names of those proficient with basic comprehension, but should work on standards:** **Student names of those that are fluent, but struggle with basic comprehension (they also need standards work):**	**Column 2: Fluency needed – accurate and slow** Students in this column have basic phonics skills, but read slowly. **For students in this column, complete the universal screener:** ♦ Example: Oral reading fluency between 25th and 39th percentiles ♦ Example: Composite score between 25th and 39th percentiles **Next steps:** ♦ To be in this column, phonics must be ruled out as a barrier to fluency. A phonics survey should be completed. If this survey reveals holes in phonics mastery, the student should be moved to Column 3. **Fluency skills to consider:** _____Reads word by word _____Reads with some phrasing _____Speed reads the passage _____Adjusts rate for comprehension _____Rate impacts accuracy **Possible intervention (example):** ♦ Read Naturally **Your intervention tools here:** **Student names:**

(continued overleaf)

Continued

Column 3: Phonics needed, possibly phonological awareness	Column 4: Phonics needed, phonological awareness needed
Students in this column need direct, explicit instruction in phonics skills and in application of phonics in connected text.	Students in this column need direct, explicit instruction in phonics and phonological awareness.
For students in this column, complete the universal screener: ♦ Example: Oral reading fluency between 11th and 24th percentiles ♦ Example: Composite score between 11th and 24th percentiles ♦ Students in Column 2 found to have phonics concerns as determined by a phonics survey **Next steps:** ♦ Complete the phonics survey to pinpoint where students are in the scope and sequence of phonics ♦ Complete the phonological awareness diagnostic to rule out a phonological deficit OR confirm the deficit to determine the instructional focus **Possible interventions (examples):** ♦ Phonics: Sound Partners; Fundations ♦ Phonological awareness: Heggerty; www.fcrr.org (match need to areas of deficit on the phonological awareness survey); LiPS **Your intervention tools here:** **Student names – phonics only:** **Student names – phonics and phonological awareness:**	**For students in this column, complete the universal screener:** ♦ Example: Oral reading fluency below 10th percentile ♦ Example: Composite score below 10th percentile **Next steps:** ♦ Complete the phonics survey to pinpoint where students are in the scope and sequence of phonics – identify the instructional focus ♦ Complete the phonological awareness diagnostic to identify needs within the scope and sequence of phonological awareness ♦ It is possible students in this column could pass the phonological awareness diagnostic. If they do, they will only require phonics intervention **Possible interventions (examples):** ♦ Phonics: Sound Partners; Fundations; Wilson Reading System; Barton Reading; Orton-Gillingham ♦ Phonological awareness: Heggerty; www.fcrr.org (match need to areas of deficit on the phonological awareness diagnostic); LiPS **Your intervention tools here:** **Student names – phonics only:** **Student names – phonics and phonological awareness:**

Second Through Fifth Grade Columns
Second Grade Answer Key

Column 1: Comprehension/standards work needed – students are fluent and accurate Students in this column have phonics, are fluent readers, but need to continue to work on grade level standards. **For students in this column, complete the universal screener:** ◆ Example: AIMSweb oral reading at/above 40th percentile **To identify the instructional focus:** ◆ Common formative assessments aligned to state standards **Possible enrichments/interventions:** ◆ Standards work-identified prioritized standards ◆ Student's next steps may be enrichment related to the standards OR it could be intervention on basic comprehension plus standards work **Student names of those proficient with basic comprehension, but should work on standards:** ◆ William 84% ◆ James 52% ◆ Aliyah 75% ◆ DeShawn 99% ◆ Cole 81% **Student names of those that are fluent, but struggle with basic comprehension (they also need standards work):** ◆ Ebony 42% ◆ Brett 40%	**Column 2: Fluency needed – accurate and slow** Students in this column have basic phonics skills, but read slowly. **For students in this column, complete the universal screener:** ◆ Example: AIMSweb oral reading between 25th and 39th percentiles **Next steps:** ◆ To be in this column, phonics must be ruled out as a barrier to fluency. A phonics survey should be completed. If this survey reveals holes in phonics mastery, the student should be moved to Column 3 **Fluency skills to consider:** _____Reads word by word _____Reads with some phrasing _____Speed reads the passage _____Adjusts rate for comprehension _____Rate impacts accuracy **Possible intervention (example):** ◆ Read Naturally **Your intervention tools here:** **Student names:** ◆ Ava ◆ Stella

(continued overleaf)

Continued

Column 3: Phonics needed, possibly phonological awareness	Column 4: Phonics needed, phonological awareness needed
Students in this column need direct, explicit instruction in phonics skills and in application of phonics in connected text.	Students in this column need direct, explicit instruction in phonics and phonological awareness.
For students in this column, complete the universal screener: ◆ AIMSweb oral reading between 11th and 24th percentiles ◆ Students in Column 2 found to have phonics concerns as determined by a phonics survey ◆ Complete the phonics survey to pinpoint where students are in the scope and sequence of phonics ◆ Complete the phonological awareness diagnostic to rule out a phonological deficit OR confirm the deficit to determine the instructional focus	**For students in this column, complete the universal screener:** ◆ AIMSweb oral reading below 10th percentile ◆ Complete the phonics survey to pinpoint where students are in the scope and sequence of phonics – identify the instructional focus ◆ Complete the phonological awareness diagnostic to identify needs within the scope and sequence of phonological awareness ◆ It is possible students in this column could pass the phonological awareness diagnostic. If they do, they will only require phonics intervention
Possible interventions (examples): ◆ Phonics: Sound Partners Fundations ◆ Phonological awareness: Heggerty; www.fcrr.org (match need to areas of deficit on the phonological awareness survey)	**Possible intervention (examples):** ◆ Phonics: Sound Partners; Fundations ◆ Phonological awareness: Heggerty; www.fcrr.org (match need to areas of deficit on the phonological awareness diagnostic)
Your intervention tools here:	**Your intervention tools here:**
Student names – phonics only: ◆ Mason ◆ Deja	**Student names – phonics only:** ◆ Brooklyn
Student names – phonics and phonological awareness: ◆ Ethan ◆ Nia	**Student names – phonics and phonological awareness:** ◆ Charlotte ◆ Leah ◆ Elijah

Third Grade Case Study

Data Collection Form for Third Grade

Student	Universal Screening Percentile for Oral Reading or Composite Score	Basic Comprehension or Standards Work (Column 1)	Phonological Awareness Diagnostic *Areas of deficit	Phonics Survey *Areas of deficit	Notes
Asia	3% (4)		Asia has deficient skills in rhyming and beginning sounds (stopped the test).	Asia does not know letter names and sounds.	Asia has needs in basic foundational skills. She needs intervention in letter names, sounds, and phonological awareness.
Luciana	24% (3) **Move to Column 2 based on phonics survey.			Given – student passed the test.	Luciana passed the phonics survey which means she does not have a phonics deficit. She should move to Column 2 and receive a fluency intervention.
Madeline	67% (1)	Standards work			Madeline is making good progress. She should continue with complex text and grade level standards.
Felipe	18% (3)		Filipe passed the phonological diagnostic.	Felipe passed letter names and sounds, but did not pass short vowels.	Felipe passed the phonological diagnostic, but needs intervention in phonics beginning at the short vowel level.
David	58%	Basic comprehension.			David is progressing

(continued overleaf)

Continued

Student	Universal Screening Percentile for Oral Reading or Composite Score	Basic Comprehension or Standards Work (Column 1)	Phonological Awareness Diagnostic *Areas of deficit	Phonics Survey *Areas of deficit	Notes
	(1)				well, but needs additional help with basic comprehension strategies.
Mateo	34% (2)			Mateo passed the phonics survey.	We gave the additional phonics survey to be sure there were no underlying skills deficits in phonics. Mateo passed this survey, so he should remain in Column 2 for additional fluency support.
Elena	77% (1)	Standards work			Elena is making great progress. She should continue working on grade level standards.
Kennedy	92% (1)	Standards work			Kennedy is making great progress. She should continue working on grade level standards.
Darnell	12% (3)		Darnell has deficient skills in phoneme segmentation and beginning sounds	Darnell passed letter names, but does not know all	Darnell is just above the cut-off for Column 4. He is a student we should watch

(continued overleaf)

Continued

Student	Universal Screening Percentile for Oral Reading or Composite Score	Basic Comprehension or Standards Work (Column 1)	Phonological Awareness Diagnostic *Areas of deficit	Phonics Survey *Areas of deficit	Notes
			(stopped the test).	letter sounds.	very closely. He should be in interventions for both phonological awareness and phonics.
Raven	47% (1)	Basic comprehension			Raven is progressing well, but needs additional help with basic comprehension strategies and grade level standards.
Sebastian	4% (4)		Sebastian has deficient skills in rhyming and beginning sounds.	Sebastian does not know all letter names and only has a few sounds.	Sebastian has very few foundational skills and needs work in both basic phonics and phonological awareness. He will need to be placed in both interventions.
Anna	42% (1)	Basic comprehension			Anna just barely made the cut-off for Column 1. She needs additional work with basic comprehension strategies and grade level standards.

(continued overleaf)

Continued

Student	Universal Screening Percentile for Oral Reading or Composite Score	Basic Comprehension or Standards Work (Column 1)	Phonological Awareness Diagnostic *Areas of deficit	Phonics Survey *Areas of deficit	Notes
Lucy	29% (2) **Move to Column 3 because there are deficient phonics skills.		Because Lucy moved to Column 3, we checked this to be sure there are not phonological deficits. There are not.	Lucy has deficient skills in vowel teams and multisyllabic words.	Lucy was initially placed in Column 2 due to her 29% screener score. When given the phonics survey, we see she has basic phonics, but needs additional practice with vowel teams and multisyllabic words. Move her to Column 3.
Marquis	37% (2)			Marquis passed the phonics survey.	Marquis is placed correctly and should remain in Column 2 for additional fluency intervention.
Manuela	33% (2) **Move to Column 3 because there are deficient phonics skills.		Because Manuela moved to Column 3, we checked this to be sure there are not phonological deficits. There are not.	Manuela has deficient skills in decoding multisyllabic words.	Manuela was first placed in Column 2 due to his 33% screener score. When given the phonics survey, we see he has basic phonics, but needs additional practice with multisyllabic words. He should move to

(continued overleaf)

Continued

Student	Universal Screening Percentile for Oral Reading or Composite Score	Basic Comprehension or Standards Work (Column 1)	Phonological Awareness Diagnostic *Areas of deficit	Phonics Survey *Areas of deficit	Notes
					Column 3 to work on these skills.
Logan	56% (1)	Standards work			Logan is progressing and should continue to work on complex text and grade level standards.
Shanice	36% (2)			Shanice passed the phonics survey.	Shanice is placed in the correct Column and should receive an intervention in fluency.

Step One

Using the second through fifth grade Columns, match each percentile score to the percentile range on the Columns. If the child has been given additional assessments, you will see that listed. This information may change Column placement.

Step Two

Create groups to determine how to place kids with needed skills together.

Column 1

Standards work:
- Madeline 67%
- Elena 77%
- Kennedy 92%
- Logan 56%

Basic comprehension and standards work:
- David 58%
- Raven 47%
- Anna 42%

**Note: Logan's score looks similar to David's, but through other assessments, you have learned that he is stronger in comprehension skills than David who scored similarly on the universal screener. The teacher will need to determine how these seven kids best fit together according to their needs. Additional assessments such as common assessments or comprehension assessments may be needed to determine this.

Enrichment: Continue to teach complex text using grade level standards; apply standards to books they are reading

Column 2
Needs fluency:
- Luciana
- Mateo
- Marquis
- Shanice

Intervention ideas: Read Naturally; Fluency Formula

Column 3
Needs phonics:
- Felipe
- Lucy
- Manuela

Needs phonics and phonological awareness:
- Darnell

Intervention ideas: Double dose of Fundations; Sound Partners Kindergarten; www.fcrr.org; Orton-Gillingham; Heggerty Phonological Curriculum

Column 4
Below 10% in phonics and/or phonological awareness

Needs phonics:

Needs phonics and phonological awareness:
- Asia
- Sebastian

Intervention ideas: Double dose of Fundations; Sound Partners Kindergarten; Wilson Reading System; Barton Reading; Orton-Gillingham; Heggerty Phonological Curriculum

**Note: It may be possible to combine students in Columns 3 and 4 when creating intervention groups. Using the interventions you have available in your school, determine where each child should start in the lesson progression of the intervention. If students in these columns fall together, it is fine to place them together. The reason we created a distinction for Columns 3 and 4 is because the teacher should pay very close attention to those students below the 10th percentile. By giving them their own column, it allows the teacher to track them closely.

Step Three

We are ready to match the intervention to the group. You will see we have given examples. Again, these are simply samples of options. Use what interventions you have available in your school. The teacher should list the interventions available and create groups, then decide who will teach this group.

Second Through Fifth Grade Columns for Practice Sorting

Column 1: Comprehension/standards work needed – students are fluent and accurate	Column 2: Fluency needed – accurate and slow
Students in this column have phonics, are fluent readers, but need to continue to work on grade level standards.	Students in this column have basic phonics skills, but read slowly.

Column 1: Comprehension/standards work needed – students are fluent and accurate

Students in this column have phonics, are fluent readers, but need to continue to work on grade level standards.

For students in this column, complete the universal screener:
- Example: Oral reading fluency at/above 40th percentile
- Example: Composite score at/above 40th percentile

To identify the instructional focus:
- Common formative assessments aligned to state standards
- Vocabulary if your screener assesses this component

Possible enrichments (top of the Column)/interventions (bottom of the Column):
- Standards work-identified prioritized standards
- Vocabulary
- Student's next steps may be enrichment related to the standards OR it could be intervention on basic comprehension plus standards work (PALS, Making Meaning, Strategies that Work Toolkit)
- Standards-based websites

Student names of those proficient with basic comprehension, but should work on standards:

Student names of those that are fluent, but struggle with basic comprehension (they also need standards work):

Column 2: Fluency needed – accurate and slow

Students in this column have basic phonics skills, but read slowly.

For students in this column, complete the universal screener:
- Example: Oral reading fluency between 25th and 39th percentiles
- Example: Composite score between 25th and 39th percentiles

Next steps:
- To be in this column, phonics must be ruled out as a barrier to fluency. A phonics survey should be completed. If this survey reveals holes in phonics mastery, the student should be moved to Column 3

Fluency skills to consider:
_____Reads word by word
_____Reads with some phrasing
_____Speed reads the passage
_____Adjusts rate for comprehension
_____Rate impacts accuracy

Possible intervention (example):
- Read Naturally

Your intervention tools here:

Student names:

(continued overleaf)

Continued

Column 3: Phonics needed, possibly phonological awareness	Column 4: Phonics needed, phonological awareness needed
Students in this column need direct, explicit instruction in phonics skills and in application of phonics in connected text.	Students in this column need direct, explicit instruction in phonics and phonological awareness.
For students in this column, complete the universal screener: ◆ Example: Oral reading fluency between 11th and 24th percentiles ◆ Example: Composite score between 11th and 24th percentiles ◆ Students found in Column 2 to have phonics concerns as determined by a phonics survey **Next steps:** ◆ Complete the phonics survey to pinpoint where students are in the scope and sequence of phonics ◆ Complete the phonological awareness diagnostic to rule out a phonological deficit OR confirm the deficit to determine the instructional focus **Possible interventions (examples):** ◆ Phonics: Sound Partners; Fundations ◆ Phonological awareness: Heggerty; www.fcrr.org (match need to areas of deficit on the phonological awareness survey); LiPS **Your intervention tools here:** **Student names – phonics only:** **Student names – phonics and phonological awareness:**	**For students in this column, complete the universal screener:** ◆ Example: Oral reading fluency below 10th percentile ◆ Example: Composite score below 10th percentile **Next steps:** ◆ Complete the phonics survey to pinpoint where students are in the scope and sequence of phonics – identify the instructional focus ◆ Complete the phonological awareness diagnostic to identify needs within the scope and sequence of phonological awareness ◆ It is possible students in this column could pass the phonological awareness diagnostic. If they do, they will only require phonics intervention **Possible interventions (examples):** ◆ Phonics: Sound Partners; Fundations; Wilson Reading System; Barton Reading; Orton-Gillingham ◆ Phonological awareness: Heggerty; www.fcrr.org (match need to areas of deficit on the phonological awareness diagnostic); LiPS **Your intervention tools here:** **Student names – phonics only:** **Student names – phonics and phonological awareness:**

Second Through Fifth Grade Columns
Third Grade Example Answer Key

Column 1: Comprehension/standards work needed – students are fluent and accurate
Students in this column have phonics, are fluent readers, but need to continue to work on grade level standards.

For students in this column, complete the universal screener:
- Example: AIMSweb oral reading at/above 40th percentile
- Example: Composite score at/above 40th percentile

To identify the instructional focus:
- Common formative assessments aligned to state standards

Possible enrichments/interventions:
- Standards work-identified prioritized standards
- Student's next steps may be enrichment related to the standards OR it could be intervention on basic comprehension plus standards work

Student names of those proficient with basic comprehension, but should work on standards:
- Madeline 67%
- Elena 77%
- Kennedy 92%
- Logan 56%

Student names of those that are fluent, but struggle with basic comprehension (they also need standards work):
- David 58%
- Raven 47%
- Anna 42%

Column 2: Fluency needed – accurate and slow
Students in this column have basic phonics skills, but read slowly.

For students in this column, complete the universal screener:
- Example: AIMSweb oral reading between 25th and 39th percentiles
- Example: Composite score between 25th and 39th percentiles

Next steps:
- To be in this column, phonics must be ruled out as a barrier to fluency. A phonics survey should be completed. If this survey reveals holes in phonics mastery, the student should be moved to Column 3

Fluency skills to consider:
_____Reads word by word
_____Reads with some phrasing
_____Speed reads the passage
_____Adjusts rate for comprehension
_____Rate impacts accuracy

Possible intervention (example):
- Read Naturally

Your intervention tools here:

Student names:
- Luciana
- Mateo
- Marquis
- Shanice

(continued overleaf)

Continued

Column 3: Phonics needed, possibly phonological awareness	Column 4: Phonics needed, phonological awareness needed
Students in this column need direct, explicit instruction in phonics skills and in application of phonics in connected text.	Students in this column need direct, explicit instruction in phonics and phonological awareness.
For students in this column, complete the universal screener: ◆ Example: AIMSweb oral reading between 11th and 24th percentiles ◆ Example: Composite score between 11th and 24th percentiles	**For students in this column, complete the universal screener:** ◆ Example: AIMSweb oral reading below 10th percentile ◆ Example: Composite score below the 10th percentile
Next steps: ◆ Students in Column 2 found to have phonics concerns as determined by a phonics survey ◆ Complete the phonics survey to pinpoint where students are in the scope and sequence of phonics ◆ Complete the phonological awareness diagnostic to rule out a phonological deficit OR confirm the deficit to determine the instructional focus	**Next steps:** ◆ Complete the phonics survey to pinpoint where students are in the scope and sequence of phonics – identify the instructional focus ◆ Complete the phonological awareness diagnostic to identify needs within the scope and sequence of phonological awareness ◆ It is possible students in this column could pass the phonological awareness diagnostic. If they do, they will only require phonics intervention
Possible interventions (examples): ◆ Phonics: Sound Partners; Fundations ◆ Phonological awareness: Heggerty; www.fcrr.org (match need to areas of deficit on the phonological awareness survey)	**Possible interventions (examples):** ◆ Phonics: Sound Partners; Fundations ◆ Phonological awareness: Heggerty; www.fcrr.org (match need to areas of deficit on the phonological awareness diagnostic)
Your intervention tools here:	**Your intervention tools here:**
Student names – phonics only: ◆ Felipe ◆ Lucy ◆ Manuela	**Student names – phonics only:**
Student names – phonics and phonological awareness: ◆ Darnell	**Student names – phonics and phonological awareness:** ◆ Asia ◆ Sebastian

Fourth Grade Case Study

Data Collection Form for Fourth Grade

Student	Universal Screening Percentile for Oral Reading or Composite Score	Basic Comprehension or Standards Work (Column 1)	Phonological Awareness Diagnostic *Areas of deficit	Phonics Survey *Areas of deficit	Notes
Bianca	65% (1)	Standards work			Bianca is scoring high on the screener. She should continue to work on grade level standards. She scored proficient on the state test.
Luna	37% (2)			Given – student passed the test.	Luna passed the phonics survey which means she does not have a phonics deficit. She should remain in Column 2 and receive a fluency intervention. Luna scored basic on the state test.
Samuel	25% (2) *Move to Column 3, based on phonics survey information.		Given – student passed the test.	Samuel did not pass vowel teams or multisyllabic words.	Samuel should be moved to Column 3 due to his results on the phonics screener. This result also triggered a check for phonological skills. He did pass this diagnostic, so only needs additional phonics work. Place him in "phonics only."
Terrance	9%		Terrance did not pass	Terrance passed letter	Terrance has deficient skills in

(continued overleaf)

Continued

Student	Universal Screening Percentile for Oral Reading or Composite Score	Basic Comprehension or Standards Work (Column 1)	Phonological Awareness Diagnostic *Areas of deficit	Phonics Survey *Areas of deficit	Notes
	(4)		phoneme segmentation, ending sounds, or substitution/deletion.	names and sounds, but did not pass short vowels.	phonics and phonological awareness. He should be placed in this section of Column 4 and receive intervention for both components.
Matthew	42% (1)	Basic comprehension			Matthew is in Column 1, but still struggles with basic comprehension. He is reading at a reasonable rate, but needs to work on comprehension. He scored below proficient on the state test.
Darius	52% (1)	Standards work			We should watch Darius closely. He falls close to the 40% cut-off. He seems to do okay on basic comprehension, so continue with standards work, but keep a close eye on him. He scored proficient on the state exam, but only by a few points.

(continued overleaf)

Continued

Student	Universal Screening Percentile for Oral Reading or Composite Score	Basic Comprehension or Standards Work (Column 1)	Phonological Awareness Diagnostic *Areas of deficit	Phonics Survey *Areas of deficit	Notes
Elly	75% (1)	Standards work			Elly is doing well and should continue to deeply develop grade level standards. She was proficient on the state test.
Allison	99% (1)	Standards work			Allison is a high-performing student. Continue to give her more complex text around standards at and above grade level. She scored advanced on the state test.
Natalia	15% (3)		Natalia has deficient skills in ending sounds, deletion, and substitution.	Natalia passed letter naming and sounds. She has deficits in short vowels, digraphs, and blends.	Natalia is just above the cut-off for Column 4. She is a student we should watch very closely. She should be in interventions for both phonics and phonological awareness.
Juan	23% (3)		Juan passed the phonological diagnostic.	Juan passed letter names, sounds, and short vowels. He did not pass blends and digraphs.	Juan should be placed in Column 3, phonics only. Match him with other students who need blend and digraph work.

(continued overleaf)

Continued

Student	Universal Screening Percentile for Oral Reading or Composite Score	Basic Comprehension or Standards Work (Column 1)	Phonological Awareness Diagnostic *Areas of deficit	Phonics Survey *Areas of deficit	Notes
Nevaeh	16% (3)		Nevaeh has deficient skills in syllables, ending sounds, substitution, and deletion.	Nevaeh passed letter names and sounds, but does not have short vowels mastered.	Nevaeh should be placed in Column 3, phonics and phonological awareness. She needs intervention in both components.
Piper	40% (1)	Basic comprehension			Piper just barely made the cut-off for Column 1. She needs additional work on basic comprehension strategies. She was not proficient on the state test.
Gabriel	88% (1)	Standards work			Gabriel is progressing well and should continue to work on complex text with grade level standards at and above grade level. He was advanced on the state test.
Victoria	38% (2)			Victoria passed the phonics survey.	Victoria is placed correctly and should remain in Column 2 for additional fluency intervention.

(continued overleaf)

Continued

Student	Universal Screening Percentile for Oral Reading or Composite Score	Basic Comprehension or Standards Work (Column 1)	Phonological Awareness Diagnostic *Areas of deficit	Phonics Survey *Areas of deficit	Notes
					Victoria was proficient on the state test. It could be that she is comprehending at a very high level, but just processing slowly. If this is the case, she may not require additional intervention.
Charles	9% (4)		Charles has deficient skills in rhyming, and beginning sounds (stopped the test because of difficulty).	Charles knows his letters, he does not know letter sounds.	Charles is in Column 4 and needs basic letter sound work and phonological intervention.
Imani	9% (4)		Imani passed the phonological diagnostic.	Imani does not know letters names or sounds.	Imani passed the phonological diagnostic, but needs letter names and sounds. She should be placed in Column 4, phonics only.
Jada	5% (4)		Jada has deficient skills in beginning sounds and ending sounds (stopped the test because of difficulty).	Jada does not know letter names or sounds.	Jada is in Column 4 and needs letter names, letter sounds, and phonological interventions.

Step One

Using the second through fifth grade Columns, match each percentile score to the percentile range on the Columns. If the child has been given additional assessments, you will see that listed. This information may change Column placement.

Step Two

Create groups to determine how to place kids with needed skills together.

Column 1

Standards work:
- Bianca 65% Proficient
- Darius 52% Proficient
- Elly 75% Proficient
- Allison 99% Advanced
- Gabriel 88% Advanced

Basic comprehension and standards work:
- Matthew 42% Not proficient
- Piper 40% Not proficient

**Note: Once a student has a score for a state test, that is one additional piece of information a teacher has. Students can at times score in Column 1, but may not be proficient on a state exam. When this happens, the teacher should examine why. Does the student need additional support with state standards? Is it test anxiety? Motivation? Stamina? There are a host of reasons. The teacher should use other information to explore why the student is not proficient.

Enrichment: Continue to teach complex text using grade level standards; apply standards to books they are reading; use standards-based websites to continue practicing grade level standards that are low.

Column 2

Needs fluency:
- Luna
- Victoria (scores proficient on state test – see notes)

Intervention ideas: Read Naturally; Fluency Formula

Column 3

Needs phonics:
- Samuel
- Juan

Needs phonics and phonological awareness:
- Natalia
- Navaeh

Intervention ideas: Double dose of Fundations; Sound Partners; www.fcrr.org; Orton-Gillingham; Heggerty Phonological Curriculum

**Note: Are kids in Column 3 ever proficient on state tests? Sure, it can happen. It is not likely though as most of these students have deficits in phonics, which means they are not able to decode well, thus making state exams very difficult. But there is always a chance they have other really good strategies. This said, even if they do score well, the teacher should work to remediate missing skills.

Column 4
Below 10% in phonics and/or phonological awareness

Needs phonics:
- Imani

Needs phonics and phonological awareness:
- Terrance
- Charles
- Jada

Intervention ideas: Double dose of Fundations; Sound Partners; Wilson Reading System; Barton Reading; Orton-Gillingham; Heggerty Phonological Curriculum

**Note: It may be possible to combine students in Columns 3 and 4 when creating intervention groups. Using the interventions you have available in your school, determine where each child should start in the lesson progression of the intervention. If students in these Columns fall together, it is fine to place them together. The reason we created a distinction for Columns 3 and 4 is because the teacher should pay very close attention to those students below the 10th percentile. By giving them their own column, it allows the teacher to track them closely.

Step Three

We are ready to match the intervention to the group. You will see we have given examples. Again, these are simply samples of options. Use what interventions you have available in your school. The teacher should list the interventions available and create groups, then decide who will teach this group.

Second Through Fifth Grade Columns for Practice Sorting

Column 1: Comprehension/standards work needed – students are fluent and accurate Students in this column have phonics, are fluent readers, but need to continue to work on grade level standards. **For students in this column, complete the universal screener:** ◆ Example: Oral reading fluency at/above 40th percentile ◆ Example: Composite score at/above 40th percentile **To identify the instructional focus:** ◆ Common formative assessments aligned to state standards ◆ Vocabulary if your screener assesses this component **Possible enrichments (top of the Column)/ interventions (bottom of the Column):** ◆ Standards work-identified prioritized standards ◆ Vocabulary ◆ Student's next steps may be enrichment related to the standards OR it could be intervention on basic comprehension plus standards work (PALS, Making Meaning, Strategies that Work Toolkit) ◆ Standards-based websites **Student names of those proficient with basic comprehension, but should work on standards:** **Student names of those that are fluent, but struggle with basic comprehension (they also need standards work):**	**Column 2: Fluency needed – accurate and slow** Students in this column have basic phonics skills, but read slowly. **For students in this column, complete the universal screener:** ◆ Example: Oral reading fluency between 25th and 39th percentiles ◆ Example: Composite score between 25th and 39th percentiles **Next steps:** ◆ To be in this column, phonics must be ruled out as a barrier to fluency. A phonics survey should be completed. If this survey reveals holes in phonics mastery, the student should be moved to Column 3 **Fluency skills to consider:** _____Reads word by word _____Reads with some phrasing _____Speed reads the passage _____Adjusts rate for comprehension _____Rate impacts accuracy **Possible intervention (example):** ◆ Read Naturally **Your intervention tools here:** **Student names:**

(continued overleaf)

Continued

Column 3: Phonics needed, possibly phonological awareness	Column 4: Phonics needed, phonological awareness needed
Students in this column need direct, explicit instruction in phonics skills and in application of phonics in connected text.	Students in this column need direct, explicit instruction in phonics and phonological awareness.
For students in this column, complete the universal screener: ◆ Example: Oral reading fluency between 11th and 24th percentiles ◆ Example: Composite score between 11th and 24th percentiles ◆ Students in Column 2 found to have phonics concerns as determined by a phonics survey	**For students in this column, complete the universal screener:** ◆ Example: Oral reading fluency below 10th percentile ◆ Example: Composite score below 10th percentile
Next steps: ◆ Complete the phonics survey to pinpoint where students are in the scope and sequence of phonics ◆ Complete the phonological awareness diagnostic to rule out a phonological deficit OR confirm the deficit to determine the instructional focus	**Next steps:** ◆ Complete the phonics survey to pinpoint where students are in the scope and sequence of phonics – identify the instructional focus ◆ Complete the phonological awareness diagnostic to identify needs within the scope and sequence of phonological awareness ◆ It is possible students in this column could pass the phonological awareness diagnostic. If they do, they will only require phonics intervention
Possible interventions (examples): ◆ Phonics: Sound Partners Fundations ◆ Phonological awareness: Heggerty; www.fcrr.org (match need to areas of deficit on the phonological awareness survey); LiPS	**Possible interventions (examples):** ◆ Phonics: Sound Partners, Fundations; Wilson Reading System; Barton Reading; Orton-Gillingham ◆ Phonological Awareness: Heggerty; www.fcrr.org (match need to areas of deficit on the phonological awareness diagnostic); LiPS
Your intervention tools here: **Student names – phonics only:** **Student names – phonics and phonological awareness:**	**Your intervention tools here:** **Student names – phonics only:** **Student names – phonics and phonological awareness:**

Second Through Fifth Grade Columns
Fourth Grade Answer Key

Column 1: Comprehension/standards work needed – students are fluent and accurate	Column 2: Fluency needed – accurate and slow
Students in this column have phonics, are fluent readers, but need to continue to work on grade level standards.	Students in this column have basic phonics skills, but read slowly.
For students in this column, complete the universal screener: ◆ Example: AIMSweb oral reading at/above 40th percentile ◆ Example: Composite score at/above 40th percentile	**For students in this column, complete the universal screener:** ◆ Example: AIMSweb oral reading between 25th and 39th percentiles ◆ Example: Composite score between 25th and 39th percentiles
To identify the instructional focus: ◆ Common formative assessments aligned to state standards ◆ Vocabulary if your screener assesses this component	**Next steps:** ◆ To be in this column, phonics must be ruled out as a barrier to fluency. A phonics survey should be completed. If this survey reveals holes in phonics mastery, the student should be moved to Column 3
Possible enrichments/interventions: ◆ Standards work-identified prioritized standards ◆ Vocabulary ◆ Student next steps may be enrichment related to the standards OR it could be intervention on basic comprehension plus standards work	**Fluency skills to consider:** _____Reads word by word _____Reads with some phrasing _____Speed reads the passage _____Adjusts rate for comprehension _____Rate impacts accuracy
Student names of those proficient with basic comprehension, but should work on standards: ◆ Bianca 65% Proficient ◆ Darius 52% Proficient ◆ Elly 75% Proficient ◆ Allison 99% Advanced ◆ Gabriel 88% Advanced	**Possible intervention (example):** ◆ Read Naturally **Your intervention tools here:** **Student names:** ◆ Luna ◆ Victoria (see notes)
Student names of those that are fluent, but struggle with basic comprehension (they also need standards work): ◆ Matthew 42% Not proficient ◆ Piper 40% Not proficient	

(continued overleaf)

Continued

Column 3: Phonics needed, possibly phonological awareness	Column 4: Phonics needed, phonological awareness needed
Students in this column need direct, explicit instruction in phonics skills and in application of phonics in connected text.	Students in this column need direct, explicit instruction in phonics and phonological awareness.

Column 3: Phonics needed, possibly phonological awareness

Students in this column need direct, explicit instruction in phonics skills and in application of phonics in connected text.

For students in this column, complete the universal screener:
- Example; AIMSweb oral reading between 11th and 24th percentiles
- Example: Composite score between 11th and 24th percentiles

Next steps:
- Students in Column 2 found to have phonics concerns as determined by a phonics survey
- Complete the phonics survey to pinpoint where students are in the scope and sequence of phonics
- Complete the phonological awareness diagnostic to rule out a phonological deficit OR confirm the deficit to determine the instructional focus

Possible interventions (examples):
- Phonics: Sound Partners; Fundations
- Phonological awareness: Heggerty; www.fcrr.org (match need to areas of deficit on the phonological awareness survey)

Your intervention tools here:
Student names – phonics only:
- Samuel
- Juan

Student names – phonics and phonological awareness:
- Natalia
- Navaeh

Column 4: Phonics needed, phonological awareness needed

Students in this column need direct, explicit instruction in phonics and phonological awareness.

For students in this column, complete the universal screener:
- Example: AIMSweb oral reading below 10th percentile
- Example: Composite score below 10th percentile

Next steps:
- Complete the phonics survey to pinpoint where students are in the scope and sequence of phonics – identify the instructional focus
- Complete the phonological awareness diagnostic to identify needs within the scope and sequence of phonological awareness
- It is possible students in this column could pass the phonological awareness diagnostic. If they do, they will only require phonics intervention

Possible interventions (examples):
- Phonics: Sound Partners; Fundations
- Phonological awareness: Heggerty; www.fcrr.org (match need to areas of deficit on the phonological awareness diagnostic)

Your intervention tools here:

Student names – phonics only:
- Imani

Student names – phonics and phonological awareness:
- Terrance
- Charles
- Jada

Fifth Grade Case Study

Data Collection Form for Fifth Grade

Student	Universal Screening Percentile for Oral Reading or Composite Score	Basic Comprehension or Standards Work (Column 1)	Phonological Awareness Diagnostic *Areas of deficit	Phonics Survey *Areas of deficit	Notes
Julieta	99% (1)	Standards work			Julieta is scoring very high on the screener. She should continue to work on grade level standards. She scored advanced on the state test.
Andrea	38% (2)			Given – student passed the test.	Andrea passed the phonics survey which means she does not have a phonics deficit. She should remain in Column 2 and receive a fluency intervention. Andrea scored basic on the state test.
Santiago	26% (2) *Move to Column 3, based on phonics survey information.		Given – student passed the test.	Santiago did not pass multisyllabic words.	Santiago should be moved to Column 3 due to his results on the phonics screener. This result also triggered a check for phonological skills. He did pass this diagnostic, so only needs additional phonics work. Place him in "phonics only." Concentrate on multisyllabic words.
Jasmine	3% (4)		Jasmine did not pass phoneme	Jasmine passed letter names and	Jasmine has deficient skills in phonics and

(continued overleaf)

Continued

Student	Universal Screening Percentile for Oral Reading or Composite Score	Basic Comprehension or Standards Work (Column 1)	Phonological Awareness Diagnostic *Areas of deficit	Phonics Survey *Areas of deficit	Notes
			segmentation, ending sounds, substitution, or deletion.	sounds, but did not pass short vowels. .	phonological awareness. She should be placed in this section of Column 4 and receive intervention for both components.
Alexus	42% (1)	Basic comprehension			Alexus is in Column 1, but still struggles with basic comprehension. She is reading at a reasonable rate, but needs to work on comprehension. She scored below proficient on the state test.
Scott	42% (1)	Standards work			We should watch Scott closely. He falls close to the 40% cut-off. He seems to do okay on basic comprehension, so continue with standards work, but keep a close eye on him. He scored proficient on the state exam, but only by a few points.
Garrett	85% (1)	Standards work			Garrett is doing well and should

(continued overleaf)

Continued

Student	Universal Screening Percentile for Oral Reading or Composite Score	Basic Comprehension or Standards Work (Column 1)	Phonological Awareness Diagnostic *Areas of deficit	Phonics Survey *Areas of deficit	Notes
					continue to deeply develop grade level standards. He was proficient on the state test.
Tyrone	99% (1)	Standards work			Tyrone is a high-performing student. Continue to give him more complex text around standards at and above grade level. He scored advanced on the state test.
Penelope	37% (2)			Given – student passed the test.	Penelope needs additional support in fluency. She scored just below proficient on the state test.
Willie	23% (3)		Willie passed the phonological diagnostic.	Willie has deficient skills in multisyllabic words.	Willie should be placed in Column 3, phonics only. Match him with other students who need multisyllabic work.
Mila	16% (3)		Mila has deficient skills in syllables, ending sounds, substitution, and deletion.	Mila passed letter names and sounds, but does not have short vowels mastered.	Mila should be placed in Column 3, phonics and phonological awareness. She needs intervention in both components.
Camila	40% (1)	Basic comprehension			Camila just barely made the cut-off

(continued overleaf)

Continued

Student	Universal Screening Percentile for Oral Reading or Composite Score	Basic Comprehension or Standards Work (Column 1)	Phonological Awareness Diagnostic *Areas of deficit	Phonics Survey *Areas of deficit	Notes
					for Column 1. She needs additional work on basic comprehension strategies. She was not proficient on the state test.
Andre	98% (1)	Standards work			Andre is progressing well and should continue to work on complex text with grade level standards at and above grade level. He was advanced on the state test.
Aria	38% (2)			Aria passed the phonics survey.	Aria is placed correctly and should remain in Column 2 for additional fluency intervention. Aria was proficient on the state test. It could be that she is comprehending at a very high level, but just processing slowly. If this is the case, she may not require additional intervention.
Jeremiah	29% (2)		Given – student passed the test.	Given – student passed the test.	Jeremiah is in Column 2 and needs additional intervention in fluency.

(continued overleaf)

Continued

Student	Universal Screening Percentile for Oral Reading or Composite Score	Basic Comprehension or Standards Work (Column 1)	Phonological Awareness Diagnostic *Areas of deficit	Phonics Survey *Areas of deficit	Notes
Emily	19% (3)		Emily passed the phonological diagnostic.	Emily knows letters, sounds, short vowels, and digraphs, but does not know vowel teams.	Emily passed the phonological diagnostic, but needs vowel teams. She should be placed in Column 3, phonics only.
Willow	17% (3)		Given – student passed the test.	Willow knows letters, sounds, short vowels, and digraphs, but does not know vowel teams.	Willow passed the phonological diagnostic, but needs vowel teams. She should be placed in Column 3, phonics only.

Step One
Using the second through fifth grade Columns, match each percentile score to the percentile range on the Columns. If the child has been given additional assessments, you will see that listed. This information may change Column placement.

Step Two
Create groups to determine how to place kids with needed skills together.

Column 1
Standards work:
- Julieta 99% Advanced
- Scott 42% Proficient
- Garrett 85% Proficient
- Camila 40% Not proficient
- Andre 98% Advanced
- Tyrone 99% Advanced

Basic comprehension or standards work:
- Alexus 42% Not proficient

**Note: Once a student has a score for a state test, this is one additional piece of information a teacher has. Students can at times score in Column 1, but may not be proficient on a state exam. When this happens, the teacher should examine why. Does the student need additional support with state standards? Is it test anxiety? Motivation? Stamina? There are a host of reasons. The teacher should use other information to explore why the student is not proficient.

Enrichment: Continue to teach complex text using grade level standards; apply standards to books they are reading; use standards-based websites to continue practicing grade level standards that are low.

Column 2
Needs fluency:
- Andrea
- Penelope
- Aria (scores proficient on state test – see notes)
- Jeremiah

Intervention ideas: Read Naturally; Fluency Formula>

Column 3
Needs phonics:
- Santiago
- Willie
- Emily
- Willow

Needs phonics and phonological awareness:
- Mila

Intervention ideas: Double dose of Fundations; Sound Partners; www.fcrr.org; Orton-Gillingham; Heggerty Phonological Curriculum

**Note: Are kids in Column 3 ever proficient on state tests? Sure, it can happen. It is not likely though as most of these students have deficits in phonics, which means they are not able to decode well, thus making state exams very difficult. But there is always a chance they have other really good strategies. This said, even if they do score well, the teacher should work to remediate missing skills.

Column 4
Below 10% in phonics and/or phonological awareness

Needs phonics:

Needs phonics and phonological awareness:
- Jasmine

Intervention ideas: Double dose of Fundations; Sound Partners; Wilson Reading System; Barton Reading; Orton-Gillingham; Heggerty Phonological Curriculum

**Note: It may be possible to combine students in Columns 3 and 4 when creating intervention groups. Using the interventions you have available in your school, determine where each child should start in the lesson progression of the intervention. If students in these Columns fall together, it is fine to place them together. The reason we created a distinction for Columns 3 and 4 is because the teacher should pay very close attention to those students below the 10th percentile. By giving them their own column, it allows the teacher to track them closely.

Step Three
We are ready to match the intervention to the group. You will see we have given examples. Again, these are simply samples of options. Use what interventions you have available in your school. The teacher should list the interventions available and create groups, then decide who will teach this group.

Second Through Fifth Grade Columns for Practice Sorting

Column 1: Comprehension/standards work needed – students are fluent and accurate	Column 2: Fluency needed – accurate and slow
Students in this column have phonics, are fluent readers, but need to continue to work on grade level standards.	Students in this column have basic phonics skills, but read slowly.

Column 1: Comprehension/standards work needed – students are fluent and accurate

Students in this column have phonics, are fluent readers, but need to continue to work on grade level standards.

For students in this column, complete the universal screener:
- Example: Oral reading fluency at/above 40th percentile
- Example: Composite score at/above 40th percentile

To identify the instructional focus:
- Common formative assessments aligned to state standards
- Vocabulary if your screener assesses this component

Possible enrichments (top of the Column)/interventions (bottom of the Column):
- Standards work-identified prioritized standards
- Vocabulary
- Student's next steps may be enrichment related to the standards OR it could be intervention on basic comprehension plus standards work (PALS, Making Meaning, Strategies that Work Toolkit)
- Standards-based websites

Student names of those proficient with basic comprehension, but should work on standards:

Student names of those that are fluent, but struggle with basic comprehension (they also need standards work):

Column 2: Fluency needed – accurate and slow

Students in this column have basic phonics skills, but read slowly.

For students in this column, complete the universal screener:
- Example: Oral reading fluency between 25th and 39th percentiles
- Example: Composite score between 25th and 39th percentiles

Next steps:
- To be in this column, phonics must be ruled out as a barrier to fluency. A phonics survey should be completed. If this survey reveals holes in phonics mastery, the student should be moved to Column 3

Fluency skills to consider:
_____Reads word by word
_____Reads with some phrasing
_____Speed reads the passage
_____Adjusts rate for comprehension
_____Rate impacts accuracy

Possible intervention (example):
- Read Naturally

Your intervention tools here:

Student names:

(continued overleaf)

Continued

Column 3: Phonics needed, possibly phonological awareness	**Column 4: Phonics needed, phonological awareness needed**
Students in this column need direct, explicit instruction in phonics skills and in application of phonics in connected text.	Students in this column need direct, explicit instruction in phonics and phonological awareness.
For students in this column, complete the universal screener: ◆ Example: Oral reading fluency between 11th and 24th percentiles ◆ Example: Composite score between 11th and 24th percentiles ◆ Students found in Column 2 to have phonics concerns as determined by a phonics survey	**For students in this column, complete the universal screener:** ◆ Example: Oral reading fluency below 10th percentile ◆ Example: Composite score below 10th percentile
Next steps: ◆ Complete the phonics survey to pinpoint where students are in the scope and sequence of phonics ◆ Complete the phonological awareness diagnostic to rule out a phonological deficit OR confirm the deficit to determine the instructional focus	**Next steps:** ◆ Complete the phonics survey to pinpoint where students are in the scope and sequence of phonics – identify the instructional focus ◆ Complete the phonological awareness diagnostic to identify needs within the scope and sequence of phonological awareness ◆ It is possible students in this column could pass the phonological awareness diagnostic. If they do, they will only require phonics intervention
Possible interventions (examples): ◆ Phonics: Sound Partners; Fundations ◆ Phonological awareness: Heggerty; www.fcrr.org (match need to areas of deficit on the phonological awareness survey); LiPS	**Possible interventions (examples):** ◆ Phonics: Sound Partners; Fundations; Wilson Reading System; Barton Reading; Orton-Gillingham ◆ Phonological awareness: Heggerty; www.fcrr.org (match need to areas of deficit on the phonological awareness diagnostic); LiPS
Your intervention tools here:	**Your intervention tools here:**
Student names – phonics only:	**Student names – phonics only:**
Student names – phonics and phonological awareness:	**Student names – phonics and phonological awareness:**

Second Through Fifth Grade Columns
Fifth Grade Answer Key

Column 1: Comprehension/standards work needed – students are fluent and accurate
Students in this column have phonics, are fluent readers, but need to continue to work on grade level standards.

For students in this column, complete the universal screener:
- Example: AIMSweb oral reading at/above 40th percentile
- Example: Composite score at/above 40th percentile

To identify the instructional focus:
- Common formative assessments aligned to state standards
- Vocabulary if your screener assesses this component

Possible enrichments/interventions:
- Standards work-identified prioritized standards
- Vocabulary
- Student's next steps may be enrichment related to the standards OR it could be intervention on basic comprehension plus standards work

Student names of those proficient with basic comprehension, but should work on standards:
- Julieta 99% Advanced
- Scott 42% Proficient
- Garrett 85% Proficient
- Camila 40% Not proficient
- Andre 98% Advanced
- Tyrone 99% Advanced

Student names of those that are fluent, but struggle with basic comprehension (they also need standards work):
- Alexus 42% Not proficient

Column 2: Fluency needed – accurate and slow
Students in this column have basic phonics skills, but read slowly.

For students in this column, complete the universal screener:
- Example: AIMSweb oral reading between 25th and 39th percentiles
- Example: Composite score between the 25th and 39th percentiles

Next steps:
- To be in this column, phonics must be ruled out as a barrier to fluency. A phonics survey should be completed. If this survey reveals holes in phonics mastery, the student should be moved to Column 3

Fluency skills to consider:
_____Reads word by word
_____Reads with some phrasing
_____Speed reads the passage
_____Adjusts rate for comprehension
_____Rate impacts accuracy

Possible intervention (example):
- Read Naturally

Your intervention tools here:

Student names:
- Andrea
- Penelope
- Aria
- Jeremiah

(continued overleaf)

Continued

Column 3: Phonics needed, possibly phonological awareness	Column 4: Phonics needed, phonological awareness needed
Students in this column need direct, explicit instruction in phonics skills and in application of phonics in connected text.	Students in this column need direct, explicit instruction in phonics and phonological awareness.

Column 3: Phonics needed, possibly phonological awareness

Students in this column need direct, explicit instruction in phonics skills and in application of phonics in connected text.

For students in this column, complete the universal screener:
- Example: AIMSweb oral reading between 11th and 24th percentiles
- Example: Composite score between 11th and 24th percentiles

Next steps:
- Students found in Column 2 to have phonics concerns as determined by a phonics survey
- Complete the phonics survey to pinpoint where students are in the scope and sequence of phonics
- Complete the phonological awareness diagnostic to rule out a phonological deficit OR confirm the deficit to determine the instructional focus

Possible interventions (examples):
- Phonics: Sound Partners; Fundations
- Phonological awareness: Heggerty; www.fcrr.org (match need to areas of deficit on the phonological awareness survey); LiPS

Your intervention tools here:

Student names – phonics only:
- Santiago
- Willie
- Emily
- Willow

Student names – phonics and phonological awareness:
- Mila

Column 4: Phonics needed, phonological awareness needed

Students in this column need direct, explicit instruction in phonics and phonological awareness.

For students in this column, complete the universal screener:
- Example: AIMSweb oral reading below 10th percentile
- Example: Composite score below 10th percentile

Next steps:
- Complete the phonics survey to pinpoint where students are in the scope and sequence of phonics, identify the instructional focus
- Complete the phonological awareness diagnostic to identify needs within the scope and sequence of phonological awareness
- It is possible students in this column could pass the phonological awareness diagnostic. If they do, they will only require phonics intervention

Possible interventions (examples):
- Phonics: Sound Partners; Fundations; Wilson Reading System; Barton Reading; Orton-Gillingham
- Phonological awareness: Heggerty; LiPS

Your intervention tools here:

Student names – phonics only:

Student names – phonics and phonological awareness:
- Jasmine

Final Thoughts about The Columns Tool

This book is a culmination of ways we have helped teachers over the years in identifying how to ensure foundational reading skills are met for students. We hope you find The Columns to be a helpful tool to assist in how to match data to needed interventions for students. By ensuring all students have solid foundational reading skills, we set them on the track to becoming proficient readers. Thank you for taking the time to understand our tool, and thank you for all that you do to ensure the students you serve receive the instruction they deserve. We are in awe of teachers every day. The work you do is not only extraordinary, but also inspiring. We hope this book gives you one more way to help your students.

In our final chapter, we will discuss things to consider as you begin to implement The Columns in your school.

9

A Guide to Columns Implementation

How Can I Get The Columns Process Underway?

You may be saying, "I can't wait to start using The Columns! How do I begin?" There are many intricacies to the process of hooking data to intervention, but by using our tool, you don't have to be an expert at diagnosing reading difficulties. The Columns will help you know where to begin. As a first step, determine the assessments used in your school. Your district assessment plan should reflect the five components of reading, universal screening, diagnostic surveys, and progress monitoring tools. Teachers often wonder about assessment administration. You may be unsure of how to give the assessments, when to give them, or who to give them to. Follow directions for administration as it is intended within the assessment. Score the assessment as it is written in the directions. Assessments lose their meaning, the validity of norm references, and links to criterion if we change how they are given. It is important to stick to the directions.

A next step is to begin to explore the intervention and enrichment options within your district. What specific materials are used for, which students should be involved, the frequency, the length of the lesson, and the number of students in the intervention can all be questions that arise. Some interventions require little training; others need extensive, on-going training. There are interventions that are researched and have a positive impact on student growth. To replicate their success, follow their guidelines for implementation. When corners are cut or changes are made in various ways by a number of teachers, success for students can drop. Again, adhere to the guidelines of the intervention. Also remember that The Columns provide a roadmap for where interventions fit. Our tool is designed for you to customize the interventions you have available to you. Once you determine the interventions in your school or district, add them to The Columns organizer.

Opposite of intervention are the enrichment materials in the district. It is important to consider the resources for all levels of performance. For example, in relation to Column 1 for grades 2 through 5, we discussed using the standards as a means to extend student knowledge. Explore the materials within your district that support standards work for those already fluent in the decoding process. See how these materials align with the rigor of state expectations and academic language of the standards. Again, remember that these enrichment materials can be added to The Columns tool to customize for your school or district.

Once you are familiar with your assessments and with intervention/enrichment materials, then it is time to put The Columns in place. You can first use them at any point of the year, but we suggest following the benchmarking period at the beginning of the year and right after the mid-year benchmarking period in December/January. Placement of students in The Columns can be updated during the semester. As the process unfolds and you gain experience with the assessments and interventions, questions may begin to become more specific on how to intervene with certain students or certain groups of students. Note that as time goes by and with continued use, you will become more adept at utilizing The Columns to diagnose a fluency problem, phonics problem, or phonological awareness concern and then hook that information to the intervention.

To become truly successful in The Columns process, continue to build your knowledge of the five components of reading. There is never a point that professional development should be finished in this area. Our students are too important. There is no one magic golden key that moves our students to mastery. We get more students to mastery by building our own knowledge and skill. Ongoing conversations with other educators and opportunities for professional development should be systematic and built into every school year. Take time out of your busy schedule to refine your knowledge of why students may have difficulty in learning to read. We have been studying the reading process for decades. We still find there is more to learn.

How Can I Use The Columns with My Team?

An individual can always use The Columns to support the enrichment and intervention cycle in their own classroom. However, many teachers find it helpful to utilize The Columns in a team setting. We have had extensive experience with multiple data team processes. We have seen various structures set forth through behavior, academic, RTI, and other avenues. The main stages in any data team cycle are to administer data, analyze data, plan, implement intervention/enrichment, evaluate progress, and adjust if needed. Data team meetings should be scheduled on a frequent basis, at least once a month; some districts schedule weekly. Longer sessions can be scheduled during fall and mid-year benchmarking cycles when more data are collected and reviewed. Special education, EL, school psychologists, reading teachers, or speech language teachers may join these meetings. Administrators should also attend. Administrators as the lead learners can support the many aspects of implementing assessment and intervention. Michael Fullan (2014, p. 55) states that "the principal's role is to lead the school's teachers in a process of learning to improve their teaching, while learning alongside them about what works and what doesn't." Support from outside consultants may also be helpful in learning how to analyze information. During this time, you may wish to discuss information related to analysis of the universal screener and diagnostic or go through examples of how to analyze data together. For this reason, we included examples for each grade level in Chapter 8.

For Administrators: Suggestions for How to Use The Columns in Your School or District

If you are an administrator and considering building- or district-wide use of The Columns, we offer some considerations for implementation. First is strengthening the knowledge of staff. Ongoing conversations through professional learning teams should be structured throughout the school year. Lynn Fuchs and Sharon Vaughn (2012, p. 198) discuss the need for "high levels of intensive and ongoing professional development for teachers related to progress monitoring, instruction, and intervention." These conversations can include the training needed for assessment administration and analysis, such as with the universal screener, the phonics survey, and the phonological awareness diagnostic. Teachers will need an initial training, and then have time to administer. This will generate data, but teachers may be unsure of how to access it or what reports mean. Beyond this point, further professional development may be needed in relation to each intervention. Again, some programs require more intensive learning and others are quicker to put into place. Further, consider support related to The Columns themselves. The Columns are a simple format to follow. Administrators do not have to be experts in the reading process to assist teachers in using The Columns as a data analysis tool. In addition to this, administrators should identify individuals that hold more knowledge in this area to help support teams new to assessment and interventions in the district. We recommend building a professional development, assessment, progress monitoring, and data team calendar in the spring before its implementation the following year. By doing this, administrators can ensure that critical conversations and training are therefore guaranteed for teachers.

It is imperative that systems initially implemented in school districts continue long after they begin. Successful districts create sustainability plans to ensure processes continue as time goes by. A sustainability plan will include how to maintain existing staff systems and continue to develop these individuals more deeply in the process. It will also address how to get yearly new staff up to speed. School planning should consider continued structured coaching and professional development sessions throughout the year. Another consideration in sustainability is a change in administration. New principals and central office staff should be made aware of the systems in the building and district, including processes such as The Columns. If frequent changes in administration occur within a school building, systems have a tendency to shift. It is better for a district to have a long-range plan of implementation for a system, such as The Columns, that new administration will be able to follow. With sustainability plans in place, a school may continue to adjust the system to meet their needs, but should maintain strong implementation for many years after initial implementation of the process.

In Conclusion

Let's get going! It is time for implementation of The Columns to begin. You now have The Columns in hand and can begin to use them as you analyze student data. We hope that our tool provides you with a clear structure for how to take initial data, find foundational reading skill deficits, and hook those data to intervention. We hope that The Columns will help you identify students struggling with foundational reading skills, and will then lead you on a path to fill the gaps for learners. Our goal is the same as yours, to help the students we see every day become skilled readers, mastering fluency/decoding of text and increasing their comprehension of what is read. Best wishes on your journey.

References

Ainsworth, Larry & Viegut, Donald. (2006). *Common Formative Assessments: How to Connect Standards-Based Instruction and Assessment*. Thousand Oaks, CA: Corwin Press.

Beck, Isabel. (2013). *Bringing Words to Life: Robust Vocabulary Instruction*, Second Edition. New York, NY: Guilford Press.

Fuchs, Lynn S. & Vaughn, Sharon. (2012). Responsiveness-to-Intervention: A Decade Later. *Journal of Learning Disabilities*, 45(3), 195–203. doi:10.1177/0022219412442150

Fullan, Michael. (2014). *The Principal: Three Keys to Maximizing Impact*. San Francisco, CA: Jossey-Bass.

Harvey, Stephanie & Goudvis, Anne. (2017). *Strategies that Work, Third Edition*. Portland, ME: Stenhouse Publishers.

Hasbrouck, Jan & Tindal, Gerald A. (2006). Oral Reading Fluency Norms: A Valuable Assessment Tool for Reading Teachers. *The Reading Teacher*, 59(7), 636–644.

Hattie, John. (2009). *Visible Learning: A Synthesis of over 800 Meta-Analysis Relating to Achievement*. New York, NY: Routledge.

The Iowa Center for Reading Research. https://iowareadingresearch.org

January, Stacy-Ann A., Lovelace, Mary E., Foster, Tori E., & Ardoin, Scott P. (2017). A Comparison of Two Flashcard Interventions for Teaching Sight Words to Early Readers. *Journal of Behavioral Education*, 26, 151–168. doi:10.1007/s10864-016-9263-2

Kilpatrick, David A. (2015). *Essentials of Assessing, Preventing, and Overcoming Reading Difficulties*. Hoboken, NJ: John Wiley & Sons.

Kilpatrick, David A. (2016). *Equipped for Reading Success*. Syracuse, NY: Casey and Kirsch Publishers.

National Institute of Child Health and Human Development. (2000). *Report of the National Reading Panel. Teaching Children to Read: An Evidence-Based Assessment of the Scientific Research Literature on Reading and Its Implications for Reading Instruction: Reports of the Subgroups* (NIH Publication No. 00-4754). Washington, DC: U.S. Government Printing Office.

Rasinski, Timothy. (2017). Readers Who Struggle: Why Many Struggle and a Modest Proposal for Improving Their Reading. *The Reading Teacher*, 70(5), 519–524.

Shaywitz, Sally. (2005). *Overcoming Dyslexia: A New and Complete Science-Based Program for Reading Problems at Any Level*. New York, NY: Vintage Books, Random House.

Sparks, Dennis. (2007). *Leading for Results: Transforming Teachers, Learning, and Relationships in Schools*, Second Edition. Thousand Oaks, CA: Corwin Press, 179–184.

Texas Education Agency. (2002). https://tea.texas.gov/

Instructional and Assessment References

95 Percent Group. www.95percentgroup.com/ (intervention materials)
Acadience Reading. https://acadiencelearning.org/acadiencereading.html
aimswebPlus. www.pearsonassessments.com/professional-assessments/digital-solutions/aimsweb/about.html
Barton Reading and Spelling System. https://bartonreading.com/
CommonLit. www.commonlit.org
Diagnostic Decoding Surveys. www.reallygreatreading.com/dds
EdCite. www.edcite.com/
Evaluate. https://catapultlearning.com/programs/instruction/assessment/
Fast Bridge. www.fastbridge.org/solutions/solutions-screening/
Florida Center for Reading Research. Florida State University. http://fcrr.org
Freckle. www.freckle.com/
Fuchs, Douglas. (2013). *Peer Assisted Learning Strategies: Reading Methods for Grades 2-6*. Nashville, TN: Vanderbilt University.
Fundations. Wilson Language Training Corporation, 2005.
Galileo. www.ati-online.com/GalileoK12/K12-assessment.php
Harvey, Stephanie & Goudvis, Anne. (2016). *The Comprehension Toolkit*, Second Edition. Portsmouth, NH: Heinemann.
Heggerty, Michael & Alisa VanHekken. (2017). *Phonemic Awareness: The Skills that They Need to Help Them Succeed: A 35 Week Curriculum of Daily Phonemic Awareness Lesson Plans*. Literacy Resources, Inc.
iReady. www.curriculumassociates.com/products/i-ready.
Kilpatrick, David A. (2016). *Equipped for Reading Success*. Syracuse, NY: Casey and Kirsch Publishers. (Phonological Awareness Screening Test, pp. 237–245).
Lindamood Phoneme Sequencing® Program for Reading, Spelling, and Speech (LiPS®). http://lindamoodbell.com/program/lindamood-phoneme-sequencing-program
Making Meaning. www.collaborativeclassroom.org/programs/making-meaning/

Mastery Connect. www.masteryconnect.com/

Newsela. https://newsela.com/

Phonics Screener for Intervention. www.95percentgroup.com/products/assessments

Phonological Screener for Intervention. www.95percentgroup.com/products/assessments

Quick Phonics Screener. www.readnaturally.com/product/quick-phonics-screener

Reading A-Z. www.readinga-z.com

Read Naturally. www.readnaturally.com/

Vadasy, Patricia F. (2005). *Sound Partners: A Tutoring Program in Phonics-Based Early Reading.* Boston, MA: Sopris West Educational Services.

For Product Safety Concerns and Information please contact our EU
representative GPSR@taylorandfrancis.com
Taylor & Francis Verlag GmbH, Kaufingerstraße 24, 80331 München, Germany

www.ingramcontent.com/pod-product-compliance
Lightning Source LLC
Chambersburg PA
CBHW080846020526

44115CB00034B/2941